Undeniable Proofs

The Bible is God-Inspired

by
Rev. Dennis R. Lee

FIRST PRINTING, APRIL 1999
Printed in the United States of America

ISBN # 0-89826-085-X

Dedicated to Jesus

My Savior and Lord, who after coming to him with a repenting heart, met me and carried me over to salvation and into eternal life.

I am forever grateful for you taking a drug and alcohol addicted wordly man and presenting to me a heart of flesh and a changed life.

Thank you Holy Spirit for empowering me with love, compassion, and strength to do the work of the Father.

Special Thanks

To my wife Connie, who strives so hard to be the kind of wife the scripures instructs her to be.

I know better than anyone else, that it is not always easy at times. No matter the circumstances, she's always there, loving and encouraging me.

Thank you for giving me the time and encouragement needed to complete this work of God.

Ecclesiastes 9:9
"LIVE JOYFULLY WITH THE WIFE WHOM THY LOVEST ALL THE DAYS OF THE LIFE OF THY VANITY; WHICH HE HATH GIVEN THEE UNDER THE SUN, ALL THE DAYS OF THY VANITY; FOR THAT IS THY PORTION IN THIS LIFE."

All due to your love and commitment to our Lord and me, my life is complete.

Special Thanks

To my sweet dear mother Jeanette Nance Jackson who taught me to love and fear God and whose prayers were answered when I accepted Christ into my life.

Thanks also to my sons: Dennis Scot Lee, Airman James Christopher Howard, and our "special" child Jeremy Craig Howard. God has really blessed my wife and me with some of the finest children I've ever known. Praise God all three of our sons have accepted Jesus as Savior and Lord. They have brought us nothing but pleasure. They are all three caring and responsible adults that truly do honor their parents.

All three have contributed in their own special ways with their own special God given talents toward the publishing of this work of God.

In Memory of:

Ada Noojin Nance, 1912-1993
A very loving grandmother who continually prayed for all her family. I think the Lord revealed unto me that it was the desire of her heart that someone out of her loins would some day preach the gospel.

Special Friend:

Don Audy
A brother who was converted while in prison, serving time for drug trafficking. Don was a man who loved Jesus as much as any man I've ever known.

Don was walking proof of the power of the gospel to change lives, to be born again. After accepting Jesus as Savior and Lord, he never looked back. He dedicated his life in servitude to Jesus and his fellow inmates while still in prison and after his release until his death.

Table of Contents

Introduction

The intent of this book is to prove to the atheist, agnostic, and any believer in God, whether Christian or not, that the Holy Bible is the undeniable, indisputable, and absolute word of God!!!

This work will prove that every book, chapter, verse, and word is God inspired. This work will also prove that all 26 writers were under the anointing and direction of God's Holy Spirit.

There are numerous historic, prophetic, and scientific proofs that exist throughout the scriptures that prove the Bible has an origin that's far beyond man's capabilities to produce. This work of God offers proof that is absolutely so astonishing, that no room is left for contradiction.

> 2 Timothy 3:16
> "ALL SCRIPTURES IS GIVEN BY INSPIRATION OF GOD, AND IS PROFITABLE FOR DOCTRINE, FOR CORRECTION, FOR INSTRUCTION IN REIGHTEOUSNESS."

Chapter 1
Case for Creation

The vast majority of the Old Testament was preordained for us by God in the ancient Hebrew language. The Hebrew people did not posses a numeric system as did the Arabics. So for mathematical purposes they utilized their alphabetical letters as a substitution for numerals.

For example, the first Hebrew alphabetical letter "ALEPH" equaled "1". The second letter "BEYTH" equaled "2". The third letter "GIYMEL" stood for "3" and so on.

Hebrew			Greek		
1.	א	— 1	1.	α	— 1
2.	ב	— 2	2.	β	— 2
3.	ג	— 3	3.	γ	— 3
4.	ד	— 4	4.	δ	— 4
5.	ה	— 5	5.	ε	— 5
6.	ו	— 6	6.	ζ	— 7
7.	ז	— 7	7.	η	— 8
8.	ח	— 8	8.	θ	— 9
9.	ט	— 9	9.	ι	— 10
10.	י	— 10	10.	κ	— 20
11.	כ	— 20	11.	λ	— 30
12.	ל	— 30	12.	μ	— 40
13.	מ	— 40	13.	ν	— 50
14.	נ	— 50	14.	ξ	— 60
15.	ם	— 60	15.	ο	— 70
16.	ע	— 70	16.	π	— 80
17.	פ	— 80	17.	ρ	— 100
18.	צ	— 90	18.	σ	— 200
19.	ק	— 100	19.	τ	— 300
20.	ר	— 200	20.	υ	— 400
21.	ש	— 300	21.	φ	— 500
22.	ת	— 400	22.	χ	— 600
			23.	ψ	— 700
			24.	ω	— 800

Numeric Representations

Throughout the scriptures God uses numerics in very interesting and versatile ways. Furthermore, some folks believe strongly that numerics have deep symbolic spiritual meanings.

1   unity
2   separation or witness
3   Godhead
4   creative work
5   grace
6   man (under sin)
7   spiritual perfection or completion
8   resurrection or new beginning
9   finality
10 ordinal perfection
11 disorganization
13 sin or rebellion
37 living word of God
40 probation

God binds and links scriptures with numerics throughout the entire Bible. Those revealed below are few in comparison to those that actually exist throughout the scriptures.

-seven churches of Revelation

-seven seals (Rev. 5:5-8)

-the lamb that opens the seven seals has seven eyes and seven horns (Rev. 5:6)

-seven trumpets of judgment (Rev. 8:2-11:13)

-seven vials of wrath (Rev. 15:6-6:21)

-Naaman's seven dips in the Jordan (2 Kings chapter 5)

-seven days of walking around Jericho (Joshua chapter 6)

-Old Covenant given after 40 days fast of Moses

-New Covenant given after 40 day fast of Jesus

-forty year journey for Israelites in the wilderness

-twelve tribes of Israel

-twelve disciples of Jesus

Numerics of Genesis 1:1

God in His omniscience and infinity has expounded another way for us to be expertly enriched through numerics.

If every Hebrew letter assumes the guise of a numeral, then every letter of course, will have a numeric value, so then will every word, sentence, verse, chapter, book, and even the entire Old Testament.

"IN THE BEGINNING GOD CREATED THE HEAVEN AND THE EARTH."

13

-The Hebrew words for the three main nouns in this verse are "ELOHIYM" "SHAMAYIM" and "ERETS" respectively God, Heaven, and Earth. These three words have a numeric value of "777" (111x7).

-The Hebrew verb for "created" has a numeric value of 203 (7x29)

-The "the's" have a numeric value of 406 (7x58)

-The words in between the first and last words have 896 (7x128) for their value.

Furthermore:

-The first and last letters of all seven words of Gen. 1:1 have a combined value of 1,393 (7x199).

-The first and last letters of the first and last words have a combined value of 497 (7x71).

-The combined value of the first, middle, and last letters of Gen. 1:1 is 133 (7x19).

There are over thirty documented numeric schemes in just Genesis 1:1 alone.

Even if ancient men could, why would they insert such mathematical phenomena and keep it secret for the rest of their lives?

Mathematics in our generation is just one more superb tool that God has chosen to validate that every word,

jot, and tittle of his precious word is inspired and ordained of Him.

Numeric values for alphabetical letters are not the only
way that God has procured a mathematical procedure
to demonstrate to an unbelieving world and sometimes
church, that the Holy Bible is the "TRUTH OF TRUTHS."

-Genesis 1:1 contains seven words with 28 letters
(7x4).

-God, Heaven, and Earth have 14 Hebrew letters
(7x2).

-The first three words; the subject and predicate,
"IN THE BEGINNING GOD CREATED" have 14
Hebrew letters (7x2).

-The fourth and fifth words "THE HEAVENS," have
seven Hebrew letters.

-The sixth and seventh words "THE EARTH," have
seven Hebrew letters.

-The last four words, the object of the sentence "THE
HEAVENS AND THE EARTH," have 14 Hebrew letters (7x2).

Isaiah 55:9
"FOR AS THE HEAVENS ARE HIGHER THAN THE
EARTH, SO ARE MY WAYS HIGHER THAN YOUR
WAYS, AND MY THOUGHTS THAN YOUR
THOUGHTS."

Genesis 1:1 Multiples of 4 and 37

God in his infinite complexity and incomprehensible sovereignty has not only mandated the use of the number 7 in Gen. 1:1, but includes the numbers 4 and 37 as thus.

-Numbers of Hebrew letters 28 (7x4)

-First four words have 16 Hebrew letters (4x4).

-Last three words have 12 Hebrew letters (4x3).

-the three words in between the seven words 3rd, 4th, and 5th have 12 Hebrew letters (4x3).

-The first, middle, and last words also have 12 Hebrew letters (4x3).

-The first two and last two words have 16 Hebrew letters (4x4).

-Also all the remaining words have 16 Hebrew letters (4x4)

Multiples of 37

-Words 1-5 have a numeric value of 1,998 (37x54)

-Words 6-7 have a numeric value of 703 (37x19)

-Word 6 has a numeric value of 407 (37x11).

-Word 7 has a numeric value of 296 (37x8).

-The phrase "AND THE EARTH," has a numeric value of 296 (37x8).

-Remember "GOD, HEAVEN, and EARTH" have a numeric value of "777" which is also a multiple of 37 (37x21).

-Moreover the entire numeric value of Genesis 1:1 is 2,701 (37x73).

When a group of astonished and evidently impressed math professors at Harvard University discovered that the ancient Hebrew manuscripts contain such sophisticated mathematical formulations they attempted the same process, unifying English alphabetical letters with numeric figures.

Even with taking advantage of some of today's most advanced computers, plus considering the fact they had over 400,000 modern English words from which to choose, compared to the only around 4500 ancient Hebrew words, they, despite these facts, couldn't produce but just a few numeric schemes.

The only stipulation required in their work was that they were to be stewards of only one self-chosen subject. After many humiliating pages, their feeble attempts fell to folly when you compare to what God accomplished in just the first verse of his inspiring and unadulterated word.

By challenging the authenticity of God's anointed Holy Word, they only proved with an overshadowing doubt that no ancient man could have articulated such innovated and intricate workmanship without the guiding hand of a supreme artificer that supersedes all our modern technology. That supreme artificer is the same that created all that we can see and even what our arduous eyes desire to see, the unending universe to the depths of the seas. HE is the great I AM.

Job 38:33
"KNOWEST THY THE ORDINANCES OF HEAVEN? CANST THOU SET THE DOMINION THEREOF IN THE EARTH."

Job 38:16
"HAS THOU ENTERED INTO THE SPRINGS OF THE SEA? OR HAST THOU WALKED IN THE SEARCH OF THE DEPTH?"

Odds of Random Chances

No doubt, by now inquiring minds are beginning to contemplate the odds of these complex and converting mathematical exposé's being just happenstance. Are they unrebukeably unleashed from the mind of "JEHOVAH ELOHIM"—the eternal creator?

Let's examine the possibility that all this happened randomly. By the law of averages for a number to appear as a multiple of 7; there is one in a seven chance. To calculate the chance of two numbers appearing as a multiple of 7, would be 7^2 (power) or one in 49 or 7x7.

For three numbers appearing as multiples of 7 the odds would be one in 343 or (7x7x7) or 7^3 and so on.

For the thirteen multiples of seven in Gen. 1:1 already displayed in this chapter, the odds are 7^{13} or one in 968,890,104,110.

Then add in the odds of the seven multiples of 4 or 4^7 or one in 16,384.

Finally compute and include the odds for the seven multiples of 37, one in 949,318,771,310.

Steadfastly keeping in mind this showcase of numeric features in Gen. 1:1, in this chapter, are short of complete. We have a grandeur total of one in 1,918,208,891,804.

In the beginning God "CREATED," the Hebrew word for create is "bara," which means to make, create, or manifest.

Now that it is well established that the first verse of the Bible had to be undeniably written by an intellect astronomically higher than man. The case for creation should be dramatically exhorted and investigated as has been with the theory of evolution over the last hundred and fifty years or so.

Simple Cell

Psalm 139:14
"I WILL PRAISE THEE, FOR I AM FEARFULLY AND WONDERFULLY MADE; MARVELOUS ARE THY WORKS; AND THAT MY SOUL KNOWETH RIGHT WELL."

I'm amazed at the knowledge we have obtained in re-
cent years. The more we learn though, the more we see
we have to learn. For instance, we've discovered there's
no such "excuse the pun," animal as the simple cell.
Evolutionary scientists would have us to believe that
all life came from a simple cell similar to the amoebae.
The amoebae in no wise is simple, it sports chromosomes,
DNA, and genes. This simple cell literally contains thousands of different chemicals that must not interact. Each
chemical has it's own thing to do in it's own timing. If
any of these chemicals converge or loses it's timing se-
quence, then the entire cell will die. Each simple cell
embodies about 10^{12} worth of information, enough to
fill about 100,000 pages of the Brittanica Encyclopedia.

Human Body

The human body contains over 100 trillion cells and
various chemicals. To name a few; iron, sugar, salt, car-
bon, iodine, lime, calcium, and phosphorous. God has
framed us with 263 bones, plumbed us with 970 miles
of blood vessels, created us with 400 tongue cups, 20,000
ear hairs necessary to hear, 3,500 sweat tubes to each
square inch of skin (or about 40 miles) of tubing for a
cooling system, 20,000,000 mouths that suck food as it
passes through the intestines, 600,000,000 air cells of
the lungs that inhales 2,400 gallons of air daily, a heart
that pumps 12 tons of blood daily, and an apparatus
called a brain that would diligently discomfit any human rival computer.

The Universe

Psalms 19:1
"THE HEAVENS DECLARE THE GLORY OF GOD
AND THE FIRMAMENT SHEWETH HIS HANDY-
WORK."

With the placement of our modern celestial Hubble
Telescope, God is truly being glorified. We've just simply
discovered billions of galaxies like our own that contain
billions of stars much like our own sun.

We have for years known that near countless factors
must congeal for life here on earth to exist as we know
it. An absolute necessity is the right percentage of oxy-
gen in relation to other atmospheric chemicals, evapo-
ration for clean water, distance of earth from the sun,
earth rotation and tilt must be timely and precise, the
moon controlling the cleansing tides, and etc.

Recently however, through this spectacular invention,
God and science have enabled us to understand there
are innumerable factors that have to jell, that are far
beyond our planet for life to exist on this cosmic speck
we call Earth. For instance, if one star is too close to
another the gravitational pull would be too strong for life
as we know it. As a matter of fact entire galaxies can be
too close to each other, causing gravitational pulls that
would prevent life in either galaxy.

The galaxies nearest our galaxy and the stars nearest
the Earth are proportional in number and precise in distance for life to exist her on Earth.

Furthermore, if Jupiter and Saturn weren't a part of
our Solar System, Earth would be bombarded
consistantly with meteorites. Jupiter is 1,400 times the

size of earth and Saturn is 1,100 times larger. The huge mass of these two planets produces an Earth saving gravitational pull on comets and meteors that has kept us out of extinction for thousands of years.

There's no place in the universe we could go that doesn't exploit God's omniscience and excellency. There's proof of His existence in everything and in everyone. In this age of knowledge, as prophesied, we are truly just beginning to understand the meaning of the word "omniscience." Our exploration of knowledge is really just still in it's infancy and we still have many more unanswered questions than solidly understood facts.

One thing though, for certain, we have ascertained enough to clearly perceive that everything created was by design. The more we learn the more we see the tremendous and mind boggling expertise that was involved for the innumerable and miraculous gelling factors needed for the emergence and continuance of life.

So who is this expert? Is He Allah God of Islam? Is He Hindu, God of re-incarnation into animals? Is He a Buddhist, a God who would have us go through sequences of births and deaths, until we become enlightened enough to end suffering caused by the desires of life? Is He the God that the Jehovah Witness or the Mormons worship? Or perhaps this expertise comes from a far advance extraterrestrial civilization? Then who created these volatile spacemen?

No other "so-called" writings of God bear such painstaking and challenging mathematical structuring as does the ancient Hebrew and Greek manuscripts. Even the most ardent skeptics can not deny these overpowering examples of evidence. Before ending this chapter, let a few more coals be added to the fires of proof.

-First five verse of Genesis record 33 words spoken audibly from God. These 33 words have a numeric value of 6,188 (7x884).

-The initial letters of the 33 words have a numeric value of 2,401 (7x343).

-The remaining letters have a numeric value of 3,787 (7x541).

-There are 16 initial letters of the 33 words that have a numeric value of 1,281 (7x183).

-The first and last words in this audible vocabulary (arranged alphabetically) have a numeric value of 207 and 451 or 658 (7x94).

-The first and last words (in order of occurrence) have a numeric value of 911 and 13 or 924 (7x132).

-Every seventh word in this vocabulary has for it's value 2, 20, 75 and 911; for a total of 1,008 (7x144).

-1,008 has 7 factors (7x3x3x2x2x2x2) and the factors have a sum of 21 (7x3).

Chapter 2
Old Testament Proofs

No where in the Old Testament or New Testament scriptures are we ever asked by God to except his existence by faith. (Psalms 19:1), (Psalms 8:3), (Is 40:22), (Jer. 33:22) and a host of scriptures prove God's existence historically, scientifically, and prophetically as well as these recently found mathematical wonderments. It is though, by faith, we are to believe we have eternal life through the death and resurrection of our Lord Jesus Christ. Through faith we're to believe His blood was shed for the remission of our sins, that He descended into the devil's prison and demanded the keys of death and hell from a weakened and trembling Satan and that He led captivity captive. Finally we are to believe through the gift of God's most precious Holy Spirit that we can walk free from sin, effectively witness to a decaying and dying world, and lay claim to all the promises and blessings of God through prayer.

There are over 500 prophecies of Jesus throughout the Old Testament. Many of these Messianic foretellings were completely out of His control to self-fulfill. The book of Daniel (9:24-27) give us the year of His death. He was from the lineage of David, as prophesied, (Psalms 89:4), His birth place was foretold (Micah 5:3), and His flight into Egypt (as a toddler) (Hos 11:1), just to name a few of many.

Some people question or deny that He even existed, even though there are historical secular recordings of His life and ministry.

Then there are those that believe in His existence, but only as a teacher and a prophet, not as the Christ, the only begotten son of God.

The purpose of this publication is to prove undeniably the Bible is inspired, when that is done, Jesus will automatically be shown to be whom He proclaimed.

The Bible emphatically and conclusively glorifies Him as God, in addition to all the historic evidence that some are so compelled to deny.

Dr. Ivan Panin

There are over 40,000 documented pages of overwhelming numeric validations submitted by Dr. Ivan Panin. (1855-1942)

Dr. Panin was a Russian immigrant who eventually found his way to the United States as a result of the communist revolution. He was an atheist before coming to the realization of the truth and accepting Jesus as not only Savior but Lord of his life. After accepting the truth by faith, he set about, as all believers should, to read and research the scriptures.

> 1 Peter 3:15
> "BUT SANCTIFY THE LORD IN YOUR HEARTS AND BE READY ALWAYS TO GIVE AN ANSWER TO EVERY MAN THAT ASKETH YOU A REASON OF HOPE THAT IS IN YOU WITH MEEKNESS AND FEAR."

Dr. Panin was a genius and an esteemed mathematician. He spoke several languages, two of them Hebrew and Greek. Dr. Panin, was being prepared by God, just as Moses was when he tended sheep for forty ears and the apostle Paul was under the tutorship of Gamaliel (a

greatly respected and honored Pharisee teacher of Hebrew law Acts 22:3) for the tedious and devout work that
lay ahead.

With a God addicted thirst for truth, Dr. Panin desired
fervently to delve into the Hebrew and Greek texts. He
being an expert mathematician; enabled God to intro-
duce him to his life long work.

Dr. Panin, rapidly mesmerized by the unending mathematical phenomena, dedicated the rest of his days re-
lentlessly complying to the calling of God. He, being well
into his years before completing his tasks, had to en-
dure rebuke and refusal from the religious leaders of his
day. They were too quick to remind him that since the
Christian belief was accepted only through faith, his work
lacked any or little importance to church doctrine.

I believe God has reserved the unforgettable and timely
labors of Dr. Panin for our generation. The Bible teaches
a day will come when knowledge will abound (Dan. 12:4).
This generation, far more than any previous, has seen
extreme technological advances in almost every field
imaginable. Amazing are the advancements since World
War II, just a little more than fifty years ago. We live in a
complete different world than our parents and grand-
parents did. Knowledge today increases 100% every two
years.

The most influential invention of our high-tech day is
the distribution of knowledge through personal computers and the internet. The PC's that our five and six-year
old children consider toys are more sophisticated than
the computers used to send men to the moon. We de-
pend on computers for almost every thing today. Computers, of course, are pre-eminent to almost all of today's
advancements. God though, is always several steps

ahead of arrogant and prideful man. The Bible has, since the beginning, always been ahead of man's thoughts, ways, and inventions, scientifically, historically, and psychologically. The Bible, going into the new millennium, is still light years ahead of man's high tech inventions. Computers with all their capabilities are not capable of duplicating what was done in the scriptures 2,000 to 4,000 years ago.

To be euphorically astonished by this work of God, as various mathematical concepts are presented, you'll want to revel in the fact that not one of the over 31,100 verses of the Bible escape God's attention without multi-numeric multiplicity's that are comparative with Genesis 1:1.

-The total numeric value of the entire Hebrew alphabet is 1,495; the number of year Israel was under the law. (Exodus of Egypt to crucifixion).

-Total number of year from birth of Adam to crucifixion was 4,032 (7x576).

-The first word of Genesis "Brayshth," has a numeric value of 913; the last word of Genesis "B mitsrahym," (in Egypt) has 382 for it's value. Combined total is 1,295 (7x187).

-The first chapter of Genesis has 434 Hebrew words (7x61).

-There are 21 Old Testament writers. (7x3).

-The names of all these 21 writers have a combined

numeric value of 3,808 (7x544).

-The names of the law and prophetic writers have a combined numeric value of 2,993 (7x419).

-The names of the writers of the writings have a combined numeric value of 875 (7x125).

-David, accredited with most of Psalms, has a numeric of 14 for his name (7x2).

-The last two prophetic book writers names' Zechariah and Malachi, have a combined numeric value of 343 (7x49).

-Jeremiah (the name) appears in 7 Old Testament books.

-In the Hebrew language, Jeremiah appears in 7 different forms. 1. B'Yirmyahu, 2. V'Yirmyah, 3. V'Yirmahu, 4. Yirmyah, 5. Yirmyahu, 6. L'Yirmyahu, 7. L'Yirmyah.

-The numeric value of all these 7 forms is 1,953 (7x279).

-These names occur 147 times (7x21).

-Of these 147 occurrences, 14 belong to the shortest form Yirmyah leaving longer forms with 133 occurrences (7x19).

-The numeric value of all these 147 occurrences in the Old Testament is 39,865 (7x5,695).

-Yirmyahu occurs the most, 121 times. L'Yirmyah occurs the least, 1 time. The numeric value of these occurrences is 33,089 (7x4,727).

If one were to alter just one letter of these intriguing and elaborate mathematical masterpieces, then several numeric entities would be destroyed.

Matthew 5:18
"FOR VERILY I SAY UNTO YOU, TILL HEAVEN AND EARTH PASS, ONE JOT OR ONE TITTLE SHALL IN NO WISE PASS FROM THE LAW, TILL ALL BE FULFILLED."

Revelation 22:18
"FOR I TESTIFY UNTO EVERY MAN THAT HEARTH THE WORDS OF THE PROPHECY OF THIS BOOK,, IF ANY MAN SHALL ADD UNTO THESE THINGS, GOD SHALL ADD UNTO HIM THE PLAGUES THAT ARE WRITTEN IN THIS BOOK."

God is adamantly opposed to any who would tamper with his pure and undefiled word.

Hebrews 4:12
"FOR THE WORD OF GOD IS QUICK AND POW-ERFUL, AND SHARPER THAN ANY TWO EDGED SWORD, PIERCING EVEN TO THE DIVIDING ASUNDER OF SOUL AND SPIRIT, AND OF THE JOINTS AND MARROW, AND IS A DISCERNER OF THE THOUGHTS AND INTENTS OF THE HEART."

Grandeur of Proofs

The grandeur of all confirmation of the "truth" is changed lives. Howbeit, some folks starchily deny that this power is inherit with the word of God. Denouncers such as these believe the mind can have dominion even over addictive vices such as drugs, alcohol, gluttony, gambling, and sexual perversions. These people believe when someone hits "rock bottom," that sometime they can desire a change so vigorously that they can receive victory over these life threatening habitual behaviors through the power of the mind.

I personally have no knowledge or have even heard of such cases. Although, I've witnessed countless people, who with the aid of professionals, learn to live successfully for years without giving in to their temptations. The problem is, these folks are never really cured. Professionals can only help these people treat the symptoms and not the disease itself. Sadly, these struggling folks are always just one fix, drink, or binge away from back at square one.

People that draw near to Jesus with a repentive heart and mind can and do receive instantaneous conquest over most all their iniquities. Literally millions can testify to an instant metamorphous, a change from within. Furthermore, these same converts have such mastery over their former devilry that they can partake in fellowship with those that are still dying within their immoralities, and become rays of hope.

2 Corinthians 5:17
"THEREFORE IF ANY MAN BE IN CHRIST, HE IS
A NEW CREATURE; OLD THINGS ARE PASSED
AWAY; BEHOLD ALL THINGS ARE BECOME
NEW."

Opinion of the Bible

"A man has deprived himself of the best there is in
the world who has deprived himself of this (a knowledge of the Bible.)" Woodrow Wilson

"It is impossible to rightly govern the world without God and the Bible" George Washington

"The first and almost only book deserving of universal attention" John Quincy Adams

"We, the undersigned, Students of the Natural
Sciences, desire to express our sincere regret that
researchers into scientific truth are perverted by
some in our own times into occasion for casting
doubt upon the truth and authenticity of the Holy
Scripture. We conceive that is impossible for the
word of God written in the book of nature, and
God's word written in Holy Scripture to contradict
one another. Physical science is not complete, but
is only in a condition of progress." signed by 800
scientist of Great Britain, recorded in the Bodlian
Library, Oxford

"The word of God (Holy Bible) is a standard bearer
for all people, and everyone will be judged by it.

Nothing ever has or ever will compare in equality with it's sacred contents. It embraces plans for all facets of life that will ensure the charity, tolerance, and endurance necessary to maintain happiness."
Rev. Dennis R. Lee author of *Undeniable Proofs*

Rounding out this chapter, let's indulge ourselves in more industrious and indefatigable Old Testament numerics unifying the Antediluvian Patriarchs.

Genesis chapter 5:

-28 dates are used altogether in their genealogy (Births and deaths of their sons) (7x4)

-The sum of these 28 numbers is 15,750 (7x2,250).

-From creation to destruction (the flood of Noah's day) the bible gives us 21 dates (7x3).

-Add all the years the Patriarchs lived for a total sum of 8,575 (7x1,225).

-From the first birth 130 to the last death 1656 (Hebrew calendar) or 1526 years (7x218).

-Enoch was the seventh from Adam

-The Hebrew year for Enoch's rapture is 287 (7x41).

-Adding the numbers of years Noah lived after the birth of his first son with the number of years he live in total we have 1,400 (7x200).

Multiples of 13 (son and grandsons of Abraham)

-Isaac has a numeric value of 208 (13x16).

-Jacob has a numeric value of 182 (13x14).

-Joseph has a numeric value of 156 (13x12).

In the days of Daniel and the 70 years of captivity these men were connected by God, through numerics.

-Nebuchadnezzar (king of Babylon) has a numeric value of 416 (13x32).

Darius the Mede has a numeric value of 520 (13x40).

-Cyrus (king of Persia) has a numeric value of 520 (13x40).

Whether you are amazed or unconvinced, marvel that these brief examples of evidence are extremely sparsely portioned in comparison to Dr. Panin's 40,000 pages of numeric continuity.

The odds of just these for-mentioned plentiful multiplicity's materializing unorganized go beyond the computing capabilities of most modern calculators.

Chapter 3
Jesus Messiah

The New Testament was originally inspirationally written in Greek. The Greeks as did the Hebrews used their alphabetical letters to express numerals.

	Hebrew				Greek	
1.	א	— 1		1.	α	— 1
2.	ב	— 2		2.	β	— 2
3.	ג	— 3		3.	γ	— 3
4.	ד	— 4		4.	δ	— 4
5.	ה	— 5		5.	ε	— 5
6.	ו	— 6		6.	ζ	— 7
7.	ז	— 7		7.	η	— 8
8.	ח	— 8		8.	θ	— 9
9.	ט	— 9		9.	ι	— 10
10.	י	— 10		10.	κ	— 20
11.	כ	— 20		11.	λ	— 30
12.	ל	— 30		12.	μ	— 40
13.	מ	— 40		13.	ν	— 50
14.	נ	— 50		14.	ξ	— 60
15.	ס	— 60		15.	ο	— 70
16.	ע	— 70		16.	π	— 80
17.	פ	— 80		17.	ρ	— 100
18.	צ	— 90		18.	σ	— 200
19.	ק	— 100		19.	τ	— 300
20.	ר	— 200		20.	υ	— 400
21.	ש	— 300		21.	φ	— 500
22.	ת	— 400		22.	χ	— 600
				23.	ψ	— 700
				24.	ω	— 800

Luke 12:51
"SUPPOSE YE THAT I AM COME TO GIVE PEACE ON EARTH? I TELL YOU NAY; BUT RATHER DIVISION."

Jesus, the Holy Scriptures, sanctions His name above all names. (Phillippians 2:9); Satan and the United States government in our generation don't really care how we pray or which "God" we pray to as long as we don't use "that name."

Recently I attended a graduation ceremony at a major university where prayers were permitted, but, being in fear of infringing on someone's "rights," the name of Jesus was excluded. The rights that were infringed were mine and other fellow believers.

The Bible plainly states that we must ask in the name of Jesus.

St. John 14:13-14
"AND WHATSOEVER YE SHALL ASK IN MY NAME, THAT I WILL DO, THAT THE FATHER MAY BE GLORIFIED IN THE SON."
"IF YE SHALL ASK ANY THING IN MY NAME I WILL DO IT."

All religions of the world encourage living holy lives, with the exception of Satanism, of course. Living good lives is just fine with Satan. As a matter of fact he deceives millions into false religions and false ideologies as well as tempting many into wickedness and convincing others that he doesn't even exist at all.

If the scriptures are "truth" he exists. He is the fallen angel Lucifer (Isaiah 14:12-19) and (Ezekiel 28:12-19). Satan is working overtime in these last days while the church is lethargic and bias. Dissension is the primary instrument that is in usage by this murderer. Howbeit, we can only blame ourselves.

2 Corinthians 2:11
"LEST SATAN SHOULD GET AN ADVANTAGE OF
US FOR WE ARE NOT IGNORANT OF HIS DE-
VISES."

The Apostle Paul wasn't ignorant of Satan's devises,
but shamelessly too much of the church is. We are in an
age where there are more Biblical study tools and knowledge than all the previous centuries combined and that
makes ignorance inexcusable.

Luke 12:48 (in part)
"for unto whomsoever much is given, of him shall
much be required."

As warned, some churches can be more into grand
buildings and lucrative business affairs than saving
souls. Some have wandered so far away from their chief
purpose, that is "winning souls," that they are easy quarry
for Satan.

Revelation 3:18
"I COUNSEL THEE TO BUY OF ME GOLD TRIED
IN THE FIRE, THAT THOU MAYEST BE RICH; AND
WHITE RAIMENT, THAT THOU MAYEST BE
CLOTHED, AND THAT THE SHAME OF THY NA-
KEDNESS DO NOT APPEAR; AND ANOINTED
THINE EYES WITH EYE SALVE THAT THOU
MAYEST SEE."

The Greek word for counsel is "sumbouleuo" it translates to advise, recommend, deliberate. In other words,
it's time to return to Jesus.

Is He truly the Aalpha and Omega," "Chief Shepherd," "Lord of Lord," "King of Kings," "The Prince of Peace," the Lord God Almighty," Lamb of God," "Bright and Morning Star," the Resurrection and the Life," "Horn of Salvation," "Author and Finisher of our Faith," "Wonderful Counselor," "Son of Righteousness," "Word of Life," "Son of Man," "Son of God," "Light of the World," "the Way the Truth and the Life," the true "Messiah," Jesus is the Messiah or else he is a liar.

St. John 14:6
"JESUS SAITH UNTO HIM, I AM THE WAY, THE TRUTH, AND THE LIFE; NO MAN COMETH UNTO THE FATHER, BUT BY ME."

No other holy man ever made such a statement. Contemplate and meditate on and over this. If the Bible really is derived from the flawless mind of God, just as Satan and hell are real, Jesus and heaven are tangible, but, also palatable is the fact at death man shall exist eternally either in heaven or hell.

1 Corinthians 2:9
"BUT AS IT IS WRITTEN, EYE HATH NOT SEEN, NOR EAR HEARD, NEITHER HAVE ENTERED INTO THE HEART OF MAN, THE THINGS WHICH GOD HATH PREPARED FOR THEM THAT LOVE HIM."

Matthew 8:11
"AND I SAY UNTO YOU, THAT MANY SHALL COME FROM THE EAST AND WEST, AND SHALL SIT DOWN WITH ABRAHAM AND ISAAC AND JACOB

IN THE KINGDOM OF HEAVEN."

Revelation 21:10-11
"AND HE CARRIED ME AWAY IN THE SPIRIT TO
A GREAT AND HIGH MOUNTAIN, AND SHEWED
ME THAT GREAT CITY, DESCENDED OUT OF
HEAVEN FROM GOD."
"HAVING THE GLORY OF GOD; AND HER LIGHT
WAS LIKE A STONE MOST PRECIOUS, EVEN LIKE
A JASPER STONE, CLEAR AS CRYSTAL."

Matthew 10:28
"AND FEAR NOT THEM WHICH KILL THE BODY,
BUT ARE NOT ABLE TO KILL THE SOUL; BUT
RATHER FEAR HIM WHICH IS ABLE TO DESTROY
BOTH SOUL AND BOY IN HELL."

Mark 9:44
"WHERE THE WORM DIETH NOT, AND THE FIRE
IS NOT QUENCHED."

Matthew 25:30
"AND CAST YE THE UNPROFITABLE SERVANT
INTO OUTER DARKNESS; THERE SHALL BE
WEEPING AND GNASHING OF TEETH."

Once more, if the scriptures are "truth," the battle for
souls unyieldingly soars. Satan's doom is solidly and
perpetually decreed. Man has been given an opportu-
nity to over come the seducing wiles of the "father of all
lies." God himself became the ultimate and unending
sacrifice for all mankind through his only begotten son
Jesus. Out of furious revenge Satan seeks in any way

possible to discredit the name of Jesus, knowing, that by doing so, some will experience the same fate that he so ever-speedingly faces and deserves.

When Satan steals those "sower's seeds," (Matthew 13:3-23); those that do not understand and/or are deceived by him into believing there are other paths to the father) he has inflicted the only pain, that is in his power to impose on God, stolen a soul.

Every soul is ever so precious to God. When Satan does steal a soul from him, it undoubtedly breaks his heart. Imagine a child of yours being sentenced, by you, to an eternity of torture and isolation, never again able to enjoy the love that so eminently and overwhelmingly touches your heart in every special way possible.

Hell and a Loving God

Heaven is full of worship, Heb. 1:6; Luke 15:7; Rev. 4:9-11; 5:11-14; 7:9-12; 11:6-17; 14:7; and 21:24-27. Naming just these few scriptural references of many, the word of God adamantly reveals the love and admiration of his people in their exaltation of him.

Many criticize the notion that a loving God could administer such a harsh and never ending fiery incarceration. When a person dies, whatever state of mind and heart an individual departs with remains with him eternally.

Revelation 22:11
"HE THAT IS UNJUST, LET HIM BE UNJUST STILL; AND HE WHICH IS FILTHY, LET HIM BE FILTHY STILL; AND HE THAT IS RIGHTEOUS STILL, LET HIM BE RIGHTEOUS ; AND HE THAT

IS HOLY, LET HIM BE HOLY STILL"

Anyone who hates God and his ways, and loves the world, is full of pride, rebellion, and self exaltation could never be happy in heaven with all the love, praise, and worship going one.

Furthermore, if the world hates us Christians now in our imperfections imagine the level of detestation when we are made perfect.

Jesus is standing at your heart's door, Rev. 3:20, waiting for your invitation. It's your choice, either you choose Him or Satan, by not making a choice, you involuntarily choose to remain unjust and filthy still, maybe even for an eternity.

Don't let Satan rob you of your heavenly inheritance. Believe in and on Jesus, He is for real.

If the over 500 Old Testament prophecies and previously presented mathematical displays aren't enough to convince you to abandon your skepticism, then further contemplate these grandiloquent mathematical gems.

Genealogy of Christ

Matthew 1:1-11
(Abraham to Babylon captivity)

  -49 words (7x7)

  -First three words have 21 letters (7x3)

  -Last four words have 28 letters (7x4)

  -28 words begin with vowels (7x4); and 21 words

begin with consonants (7x3).

-In the 49 words there are 140 letters that are vowels (7x20); and 126 letters are consonants (7x18).

-266 letters (7x38)

-42 nouns (7x6).

-56 nouns in entire genealogy (7x8).

-35 proper names (7x5).

-28 of the proper names are male ancestors of Christ
(7x4).

-7 women are named.

-7 common nouns; brother, king, book, birth, re-
moval, Son, and Christ.

-Entire genealogy has a numeric value of 42,364
(7x6,052).

The bible proclaims we are all pre-destined; that God
knew us before we were born. If any of Jesus' ancestors
had not been named exactly as they were, then almost
none of these mathematical gems could exist.

Angel's Vocabulary

Examine these mathematical gems implanted into the
vocabulary of the angel announcing the birth of Jesus to

Joseph.

Matthew 1:18-25

-161 words in all (7x23)

-77 vocabulary words (7x11).

-Numeric value of the 77 words is 51,247 (7x7,321).

-The first word of the vocabulary has a numeric value of 770 (7x110).

-Total numeric value of Matthew 1:18-25 is 93,394 (7x13,342).

-42 words in these passages rare found no where else in the New Testament (7x6).

-These 42 words have 126 letters (7x18).

-There are six words with 56 letters that are found nowhere else in Matthew (7x8).

-These six words have a numeric value 5,005 (7x715).

The boundless diversified mind of God.

Multiple's of 11 in the angel's vocabulary.

-44 of the 77 vocabulary words begin with a conso- nant (11x4); 33 with vowels (11x3).

-These 77 words contain 396 letters (11x36).

-The number of letters in the words beginning with consonants is 253 (11x23)

-The number of letters in the words beginning with vowels is 143 (11x13).

-The first word of the vocabulary has a numeric value of 770 (7x11x10).

-Of the 24 letters in the Greek alphabet, 22 letters are used (11x2).

John the Baptist

The prophecies of John the Baptist fore-telling of Jesus.

Mark 1:1-8 (Greek manuscripts)

-126 words (7x18)

-The 126 words have 427 Greek letters (7x61).

-84 of the words start with consonants (7x12).

-42 of the words start with vowels (7x6).

-There are 203 consonants total in the 126 words (7x29).

-There are 224 vowels (7x32).

-77 vocabulary words (7x11).

-42 of the vocabulary words begin with a vowel (7x6).

-35 begin with consonants (7x5).

-Verses 1-5 have 49 vocabulary words (7x7).

-Verses 6-8 have 28 vocabulary words (7x4).

-Every 7th word of the vocabulary (11 words) have a combined 56 letters (7x8).

-The longest word in the vocabulary has 14 letters (7x2).

-The 19 different letters which begin the vocabulary words have a numeric value of 2,298 (7x327).

How much more formidable should the evidence be? Could it be more astounding? Shall I waste more valuable print space on this page laying out numeric odds that go far beyond most human ability to fathom, especially when taking in consideration, only thirty seven numerical thus far evidences out of hundreds in just these few verses are presented. The verdict is in! Jesus was the Messiah, the Son of God, He is absolutely the "Truth" and He is our only connection to the Father and eternal life.

The creator of our infinite and multifaceted universe has walked the rocky mountains and ancient city streets of Israel. He brought with Him a message of love, hope, and peace for the Gentiles as well as the Jews. He gave His life for all who would believe. Through the spilling of His blood we are no longer at odds with the Holy Father. All now can enter into the "Most Holy" area. The road to all heavenly treasures and to Father God is eternally paved.

Isaiah 53:10
"YET IT PLEASED THE LORD TO BRUISE HIM; HE HAT PUT HIM TO GRIEF; WHEN THOU SHALT MAKE HIS SOUL AN OFFERING FOR SIN, HE SHALL SEE HIS SEED, HE SHALL PROLONG HIS DAYS, AND THE PLEASURE OF THE LORD SHALL PROSPER IN HIS HANDS."

Jesus was obedient even unto death, as we all should be. Sadly, though, many of us would be quick to die for Him, but are slow to live for Him. The Father instructed Him the same way He intimately desires to lead us, through His gentle, compassionate, but omnipotent Holy Spirit.

Every thing Jesus did, said, and accomplished was through the power and guidance of the Spirit, and because of His crucifixion and resurrection, our human bodies can now be used as cleansed temples for the promised Holy Spirit.

Acts 1:8
"BUT YE SHALL RECEIVE POWER AFTER THAT THE HOLY GHOST IS COME UPON YOU; AND YE SHALL BE WITNESSES UNTO ME BOTH IN JERUSALEM AND ALL IN JUDEA AND IN SAMARIA, AND UNTO THE UTTERMOST PART OF THE EARTH."

If we could only learn not to vex, quench, or grieve the Holy Spirit through sin, disobedience and ignorance the world could be won for Christ practically overnight.

St. John 14:12
"VERILY, VERILY, I SAY UNTO YOU, HE THAT BELIEVETH ON ME, AND THE WORKS THAT I DO SHALL HE DO ALSO, AND GREATER WORKS THAN THESE SHALL HE DO; BECAUSE I GO UNTO MY FATHER."

The Greek word used here for "greater" is "meizon." It translates more or larger. Imagine, if you will, if the entire Christian Church tuned their "spiritual ears" to "WIDO" Holy Spirit. think upon the unlimited, unbounded love that would flow ever so abundantly to all races and genders. Ponder such exhilaration and merriment that would turn a cruel and unjust world envious. Envision a magnificent, majestic peace that passes all understanding.

Age Old Question

I once was asked by inquiring but somewhat distressed agnostic uncle the "age old question," if there is a God, why then is there so much pain, misery, and so many starving children in the world? God gave me an answer that puts to shame all who would find excuses to remain in rebellion against Him, and here it is. If everyone lived by the word of God then there would be no hate, prejudices, wars,and starvation. The world would turn their spears into pruning hooks, feed the fatherless and the widows, love all their neighbors as themselves, would do away with war causing pride and greed, and exalt God to His rightful position, that is, above wife, children, career, and all our earthly possessions.

Only one man has ever lived the word of God to the letter. Only one man has ever been in total obedience to the Holy Spirit. Just that one man changed the world as no man ever has.

St. John 8:28
"THEN SAID JESUS UNTO THEM, WHEN YE HAVE LIFTED UP THE SON OF MAN, THEN SHALL YE KNOW THAT I AM HE, AND THAT I DO NOTHING OF MYSELF; BUT AS MY FATHER HATH TAUGHT ME, I SPEAK THESE THINGS.

Pre-destined Disciples

Just as the descendants of Jesus were pre-named and ordained, so were the disciples that our Lord so attentively and precisely chose.

Multiples of 7, 17, and 9.

-The numeric value of all twelve disciples is 9,639 (7x1,377) or (7x17x9x9).

-The disciples had nine names between them, with Simon, James and Judas being the names for more than one. These nine names have 28 syllables (7x4).

-The numeric value of the nine names is 7,021 (7x1,003) or (7x17x59) and the numeric value of the three names used twice, is 2,618 (7x374) or (7x17x22).

-The nine initial letters of the nine names have a numeric value of 782 (17x46).

-The rest of the letters have a numeric value of 6,239 (17x367).

-The first and last disciples called have a numeric value of 1,785 (7x255) or (7x17x15).

Let me remind you again that these amazing numeric displays relating to the disciples stand not alone. All the over 31,000 verses of the Bible have undeniable numeric proof.

God had a rationale for implanting these mathematical wonders all through His texts. He loves us all. He wants us to believe and accept His word for what it is, "the Truth" from the creator of the universe. He has went through great pains to show and prove to mankind that there is more to this life than the flesh. He went through even greater pains on the cross, fulfilling hundreds of Old Testament prophecies.

St. John 5:39
"SEARCH THE SCRIPTURES; FOR IN THEM YE THINK YE HAVE ETERNAL LIFE; AND THEY ARE THEY WHICH TESTIFY OF ME."

Jesus was speaking to the Bible scholars of His day. They were hardened from years of Pharisaism and Sadduceeism much like some are by erroneous doctrine, media bombardment, Hollywood impressions, and scientific exaggerations. All these things are a farce with God. It doesn't matter who you are, what you have done, or what you believe or what you have been taught, God has an open door of love for you.

Most folks are won to Jesus by a believer letting his light shine through example, or by a testimony of change, or by spine tingling anointed preaching. There are few in comparison that need persuasion by scientific means.

God wishes none should perish, 2 Peter 3:9. By all means that some may be saved, 1 Corinthians 9:22. Nevertheless, to God, those few are worth all the mathematical attention so meticulously interwoven throughout the midst of his overpowering word, even though some of these people are his most starch enemies.

> Acts 10:34-35
> "THEN PETER OPENED HIS MOUTH, AND SAID, OF A TRUTH I PERCEIVE THAT GOD IS NO RESPECTER OF PERSONS."
> "BUT IN EVERY NATION HE THAT FEARETH HIM, AND WORKETH RIGHTEOUSNESS, IS ACCEPTED WITH HIM."

Jesus (Multiple of 8)

Allow me to glorify our Lord wonderfully again through mathematics.

-The name Jesus has a numeric value of 888 (8x111).

-"The Christ" has a numeric value of 1,480 (8x185).

-Savior has a numeric value of 1,408 (8x176).

-Lord has a numeric value of 800 (8x100).

-Messiah has a numeric value of 656 (8x82).

-"The Son of man" has a numeric value of 2,960 (8x370).

-"The Truth" has a numeric value of 64 (8x8).

Any questions? You think God is trying to show us something? These absolutely astonishing and harmonious multiples of eight point to Jesus as the God chosen answer for all men. The congruence of these multiples of eight, ancestral numerics, and Old Testament prophecies, along with and most especially million's of metamorphic testimonies, leave little room for doubt. Jesus is undeniably LORD!!!

(Multiples of 13)

Revelation 12:9
"THE GREAT DRAGON WAS CAST OUT, THAT OLD SERPENT, CALLED THE DEVIL AND SATAN."

-That entire verse has a numeric value of 2,197 (13x13x13).

-Dragon has a numeric value of 975 (13x75).

-Tempter has a numeric value of 1,053 (13x81).

-Belial has a numeric value of 78 (13x6).

-Murderer has a numeric value of 1,820 (13x140).

-Serpent has a numeric value of 780 (13x60).

To close out this chapter let's marvel on these superbly untarnished New Testament mathematical wonderments.

-The entire Greek Alphabet has a numeric value of 3,999; the number of years from the birth of Adam to the birth of Christ.

-In the gospel of Mark, God, Jesus, and Lord appears 147 times (7x21).

-The numeric value of all these appearances 103,635 (7x14,807).

-Matthew chapter 2 (the childhood of Jesus, as well as the total number of words in the announcement of his birth) contain 161 vocabulary words (7x23).

-These vocabulary words contain 896 letters (7x128).

-The numeric value of these vocabulary words is 123,529 (7x17,647).

-As in the angel's announcement of the birth of Jesus and John the Baptist's prophecy of his min-

istry, the establishment of the first deacon board
(Acts 6:1-7) also contains 77 vocabulary words
(7x11).

Chapter 4
Ancient Argument

The last twelve verses of the sixteenth (last) chapter of the Gospel of Mark have long since the fourth century been subject to many heated doctrinal debates concerning their inspiration.

There are over 4200 Greek manuscripts in existence today. Over 620 contain the Gospels, and all but two retain these verses. The Sinaitic, and the Codex Vaticanus, are the two that are vacant of these verses. The Codex Vaticanus, however, does leave a blank space at the end of Mark, suggesting imperfection.

Most all Greek manuscripts are fragmented. The Codex Vaticanus is also void of Genesis 1-46; Psalm 105-137; Hebrews 9:14-13:25; all of 1 and 2 Timothy; Titus, Philemon, and Revelation. Should we ridiculously discard these anointed verses and books because of lost or decayed manuscript?

Albeit, these twelve verses are authenticated by other harmonizing and confirming scripture.

(a) The appearances of Christ of vs. 9-14 are coherent with John 21:14.
(b) The command to preach the Gospel and to baptize is given also in Matt. 28:19-20; Luke 24:47-53; and Acts 1:1-8.
(c) Signs shall follow them that believe vs 17-18; is supported by Matt. 10:1-8; 17:20; Mark 9:23; 11:22-24; Luke 10:19; and John 14:12.
(d) The ascension of Jesus vs. 19 is documented in Luke 24:49-53; and Acts 1:9-11.
There also exists extensive mathematical confirmation that Mark 16:9-20 is absolute in in-

spiration and is anointed of God.

Greek Manuscripts
-175 words (7x25).

-The 175 words have a numeric value of 103,663 (7x14,809).

-98 vocabulary words (7x14).

-These 98 vocabulary words have 533 letters (7x79).

-These 98 vocabulary words have 294 vowels (7x42); and 259 consonants (7x37).

-Of these 98 vocabulary words 84 (7x12) are found elsewhere in mark and 14 (7x2) are found only here.

-Of the 98, 42 (7x6) are used by our Lord in His address to his disciples.

-Verses 9-11 have 35 words (7x5).

-Verses 12-18 have 105 words (7x15).

-Verses 19-20 have 35 words (7x35).

-Verses 9-11 have a numeric value of 17,213 (7x2,459).

-Verse 10 has a numeric value of 5,418 (7x774).

-Verses 12-20 have a numeric value of 86,450
(7x12,350).

These highlighted mathematical schemes do not begin
to exalt all the numeric phenomena in this part of scripture. The staggering odds of just these 14 go beyond
any reasonable doubt.

Not only do mathematics prove Biblical authenticity,
but they, as here, can be used to show what was unleashed from the mind of God over what was conjured
up by Satan and fallible man.

A custom of ancient people was to seal important letters and documents with wet clay and a personal signet
to become tamper proof. God has tamper proofed His
word through the use of all embracing and voluminous
mathematics.

The Lord has ingenuously input to us a means to en-
snare all that is forgery and instituted a formula for the
test of the truth.

The so-called lost books of the Bible, the Apocrypha
writings are uninspired and were rejected by the Holy
Spirit and early church. They contradict other anointed
scriptures and have few or no coherent numeric formulations as does the accepted test.

No other self-claimed writings of God so emphatically
render such numeric designs. Would God give only one
group of believers such masterpieces of numeric accom-
plishments and leave other writings to fend for themselves? Would He even ordain so many diverse writings?

The Hebrew and Greek ancient manuscripts are the
only WRITINGS OF GOD that have possession of such
studious and remarkable validations. Our Lord is no

repecter of persons, in His eyes what's fair for the goose is fair for the gander. The many other "truths" are lies.

> Romans 2:10-11
> "BUT, GLORY, HONOR, AND PEACE, TO EVERY MAN THAT WORKETH GOOD, TO THE HEBREW FIRST, AND ALSO TO THE GENTILE."
> "FOR THERE IS NO RESPECT OF PERSON WITH GOD."

Scientific Generation

God fore-knew our generation would be a scientific people. We are consistently and scientifically searching for answers to age old questions and excepting less on faith than our ancestors. Our Lord has met this challenge through a numeric series that embodies over 40,000 pages of corroboration.

Mathematics, today, as never before, is a most complex and sophisticated field. Man has learned to utilize numerics in advantageous and various ways that have benefited all in about every area imaginable.

With the launching of our highly technological space shuttles, satellites, and voyagers; medicines, farming, communications, weather forecasting, and many other life sustaining fields have been immensely enhanced. Before the countdown comes endless hours of numeric configurations. Our space shuttles have to exit our atmosphere at the right angle, fly at certain heights, enter at a precise spot and angle. Satellites have to orbit a pre-prepared path at a pre-destined time or they are completely useless. Our out-of-solar-system voyagers launch and journey must absolutely be timed perfectly to take advantage of our sister planet's gravitational forces to continue their explorations.

As technical as all this, it pales in comparison in difficulty to what was bestowed upon the ancient texts in places such as the last twelve verses of the Gospel of Mark.

Satan's Attack

Mark 16:9-20 has been antagonistically and venomously opposed and attacked by Satan through the church, using tradition and ignorance.

Jesus cast out devils. When were literally commanded to cease this kind of ministry? Jesus laid hands upon the sick and they recovered. When were we literally commanded to cease this kind of ministry? The apostle Paul spoke in "tongues of angels," 1 Cor. 13:1. When were we ever told he and the early church only were granted this privilege?

Satan, by convincing the church these ministries are no longer anointed and sanctioned of God, that all this was just for the establishment of the early church, has delivered a devastating blow. You see if one doesn't believe, it's impossible to please God Heb. 11:6.

> James 1:6-7
> "BUT LET HIM ASK IN FAITH, NOTHING WAVERING FOR HE THAT WAVERETH IS LIKE A WAVE OF THE SEA DRIVEN WITH THE WIND AND TOSSED."
> "FOR LET NOT THAT MAN THINK THAT HE SHALL RECEIVE ANYTHING OF THE LORD."

There will be no demons cast out without faith. The sick will remain ill if we doubt and the church will remain dead.

It's so easy for us today to grab an aspirin if we have a headache. We have anti-acids when we glutton ourselves. We have pain killers for over-exerted bodies, radiation and chemo treatments for cancers, and surgeons for our worn out hearts. By no means am I advising any to disregard medical treatments and advancements. Though, sometime maybe, we are perhaps a little too quick to disregard our faith and God's promises in his word.

If any believe that the works of casting out demon spirits are no longer necessary, then he/she is truly blind and ignorant of God's word.

> 1 Timothy 4:1
> "NOW THE SPIRIT SPEAKETH EXPRESSLY, THAT IN THE LATTER TIMES SOME SHALL DEPART FORM THE FAITH, GIVING HEED TO SEDUCING SPIRITS AND DOCTRINES OF DEVILS."

In today's "show me scientifically" world, too many people have a problem believing in God, much less Satan and demons, and that's just fine with Satan. Imagine the effect of a massive deliverance of demon spirits. many would begin to believe in an afterlife. many would start to inquire about this life. Many would find the easily acquired answers. Finally, many would take that initial step by repenting and asking Jesus into their hearts.

Are demon spirits cast out today? Of course, just ask any missionary who believes and ministers in countries where witchcraft, idolatry, and sorceries are practiced. They can converse happenings that go beyond fleshly definitions and capabilities. Ask those that have been entangled in Satanic worship, that have witnessed the evil powers of Satan, lived to tell about it, and have been delivered. Ask any real man of God, who has believed and allowed himself to be bravely utilized as a vessel of power.

Confusion over Tongues

People involved in witchcraft have been asked what they fear the most. Their reply; Christians who pray in tongues. Then when asked why, it is a language that is understood only by the heavenly armies. Satan can't interpret.

Many suggest that this behavior is not sanctioned in scriptures. Some claim this activity is encouraged from the devil as a tool of confusion and deception.

Acts 19:6
"AND WHEN PAUL LAID HIS HANDS UPON THEM THE HOLY GHOST CAME UPON THEM; AND THEY SPAKE WITH TONGUES, AND PROPH-ESIED."

Acts 10:45-46
"AND THEY OF THE CIRCUMCISION WHICH BE-LIEVED WERE ASTONISHED, AS MANY AS CAME WITH PETER, BECAUSE THAT ON THE GENTILES ALSO WAS POURED OUT THE GIFT OF THE HOLY SPIRIT"
"FOR THEY HEARD THEM SPEAK WITH

TONGUES AND MAGNIFY GOD."

It's plain as the nose on your face, in these instances tongues were not devilishly devised. Even Jesus prophesied the use of tongues, Mark 16:17. Some believed that the use of supernatural tongues were prophesied 800 years before the birth of Christ.

Isaiah 28:11
"FOR WITH STAMMERING LIPS AND ANOTHER TONGUE WILL HE SPEAK TO HIS PEOPLE."

The division causing debates over tongues stems from the confusion over the tongues spoken to the overall church, that requires an interpreter be present, and be administered in an orderly fashion, with the tongues used in believers personal prayers. These types of supernatural tongues require no interpreter.

Romans 8:26
"LIKEWISE THE SPIRIT ALSO HELPETH OUR INFIRMITIES; FOR WE KNOW NOT WHAT WE SHOULD PRAY FOR AS WE OUGHT' BUT THE SPIRIT ITSELF MAKETH INTERCESSION FOR US WITH GROANINGS AND MOANINGS WHICH CANNOT BE UTTERED."

Ephesians 6:18
"PRAYING ALWAYS WITH ALL PRAYER AND SUPPLICATION IN THE SPIRIT AND WATCHING THERE UNTO WITH ALL PERSEVERANCE AND SUPPLICATION FOR ALL SAINTS."

Jude 20
"BUT YE, BELOVED, BUILDING UP YOURSELVES
ON YOUR MOST HOLY FAITH, PRAYING IN THE
HOLY GHOST."

It's easy to understand why Satan would want to be-little and undermine these last twelve power packed verses of Mark. These verses consist of some of the most damaging doctrines to his cause.

Deliverance—verse 9 speaks of His appearance to Mary Magdalene, whom Jesus cast out seven devils.

Resurrection—verse 12 speaks of His appearances to two more of his followers.

Great Commission—verse 15, the beginning of the church, preaching of the Gospel, the good news, it is done, salvation for all.

Spiritual warfare—verse 17, men issued power over him and demons. New non-understandable and con-fusing languages.

Miraculous works—verse 18, the sick healed. Miracles have turned many hard-core skeptics into believers.

Verse 19, the resurrection, his defeat through which he had to surrender the keys of death and hell, he no longer has power to imprison God's people. All can re-ceive the promise of the Holy Spirit and through His power are enabled to live holy lives.

Chapter 5
Not for Today?

The Old Testament too often is widely considered too difficult to understand, thought not valid for today, just for the Jews, and some feel it is a waste of their Christian time.

Difficulty of understanding the Old Testament is only an acquaintance of laziness. The Old Testament is a collection of 39 books that cover a great deal of subjects and has scores of characters. One must invest a substantial amount of time and effort to surmise and interpret it's valuable contents. It's a collection of books that need to be read often and repetitiously. having an understanding of historical events of the Biblical nations, a knowledge of the customs and the manners of ancient people, an understanding of God's dealings with man through his Son Jesus, and most importantly under the prayerful anointing of God's Holy Spirit give a prominent understanding advantage.

An excuse offered by some is that it's commandments and precepts do not apply to the church and therefore belittle it's importance, Albeit, there are some commandments, statutes, and precepts that applied only to the ancient nation of Israel. Although, some commandments, amazingly, were scientifically thousands of years ahead of their time. The Israelites, for instance, were forbidden to eat pork, which without proper preparation, can carry dangerous parasites. They were not to eat fish without scales and fins. Shellfish have a high cholesterol content and can carry suspected cancer causing agents. They were restricted from eating meat and dairy products together, which is hard on one's digestive system. How could these ancient people know these modern scientific findings?

The New Testament declares that the portrayal of lives in the Old Testament were given to us as an example.

> 1 Corinthians 10:11
> "NOW ALL THESE THINGS HAPPEN UNTO THEM FOR EXAMPLES; AND THEY ARE WRITTEN FOR OUR ADMONITION, UPON WHOM THE ENDS OF THE WORLD ARE COME."

Without reserve, researching the Old Testament as well as the New, will help an individual avoid painful and costly mistakes. Sin has a boomerang affect. We truly reap what we sow. the alcoholic sows a loss of mind, cancers, ulcers, heart diseases, weakened immune systems, and premature aging. The gluttonous will reap obesity, diabetes, cancers, heart diseases, and depression. Covetousness leads to greed, selfishness, bitterness, enemies, and depression. Sexual immorality transmits various diseases, and some are incurable. Acquired immune deficiency syndrome (AIDS) is lethal. Along with these grim diseases, sexual promiscuous behavior produces guilt that can be the root of many difficult struggles and mental maladjustments that can last a life time. Pride, greed, and/or idolatry has been the prime mover of most all horrendous battles and wars ever fought. Worry, which too is sin, develops into fear, gives rise to a multitude of diseases, creates stress and depression, is a thief of faith, peace, and trust; and is a tormentor that never allows happiness.

Proverbs 17:22
"A MERRY HEART DOETH GOOD LIKE A MEDI-
CINE; BUT A BROKEN SPIRIT DRIETH THE
BONES."

Proverbs 15:15
"ALL THE DAYS OF THE AFFLICTED ARE EVIL;
BUT HE THAT IS OF A MERRY HEART HATH A
CONTINUAL FEAST."

Philippians 4:11
"NOT THAT I SPEAK IN RESPECT OF WANT, FOR
I HAVE LEARNED, IN WHATSOEVER STATE I AM,
THEREWITH TO BE CONTENT."

The Old Testament is full of examples of sin induced
catastrophes. The effects of these sins not only affected
those that committed them, but the wide spread results
and consequences rippled after shocks that eventually
concluded into a complete aftermath of destruction for
the ancient nation of Israel. The nation of Israel once
enjoyed an economic prosperity that is yet to be rivaled.

1 Kings 10:21
"AND ALL KING SOLOMON'S DRINKING VESSELS
WERE OF GOLD, AND ALL THE VESSELS OF THE
HOUSE OF THE FOREST OF LEBANON WERE OF
PURE GOLD; NONE WERE OF SILVER; IT WAS
NOTHING ACCOUNTED OF IN THE DAYS OF
SOLOMON."

Imagine silver having no value. God truly blessed this
ancient chosen nation. During most of the reigns of David

and Solomon, Israel lived in obedience. God used this nation, in obedience, to be representative to the entire ancient Israeli known world. Kings and rulers came from all their regions to seek wisdom and council. Israel had the honor and respect of all the surrounding nations. Their military might was unsurpassed, and their sea going trade brought gold, cedar timbers, and other wealth to a prosperous home land.

Solomon, though, had unrepented sins which was a beginning of a downfall that culminated into an absolute reversal of conditions some five hundred years later. Israel had become a by-word instead of a channel of wisdom and knowledge. The empire of Babylon came not to seek council, but rather to conquer and were very successful. They left the once glistening and powerful nation of Israel in shambles. Instead of a marvelous economic system, a starving and oppressed people were prophetically eating their own offspring.

> Leviticus 26:27-29
> "AND IF YE WILL NOT FOR ALL THIS HEARKEN UNTO ME, BUT WALK CONTRARY UNTO ME."
> "THEN I WILL WALK CONTRARY UNTO YOU ALSO IN FURY, AND I, EVEN I, WILL CHASTISE YOU SEVEN TIMES FOR YOUR SINS."
> "AND YE SHALL EAT THE FLESH OF YOUR SONS, AND THE FLESH OF YOUR DAUGHTERS SHALL YE EAT."

Traditions of Men

Solomon allowed the traditions of men to take precedence over the word of God. Several hundred years before his reign began, God commanded the kings of Israel not to add multitudes of wives to themselves. The Israeli people were also commanded not to marry outside their race. The customs were, though, in ancient days, that when two nations came into a trade or peace agreement, if a king had a daughter she was to be a complimentary gift. The thought process being that the daughter would help bond the agreement with emotional and family ties.

To Solomon these seemingly small sins, even though knowing they contradicted God's word, must have seemed harmless enough. When his collection of wives peaked, he had seven hundred plus three hundred concubines. 1 Kings 11:3.

The Bible proclaims when Solomon was old that these wives turned away his heart after other gods. These women being from many dissimilar cultures began to demand that he establish temples of worship for their idol gods. He eventually caved in to their evil desires, breaking the first of the ten commandments.

Exodus 20:3
"THOU SHALT HAVE NO OTHER GODS BEFORE ME."

Part of the worship process of the idol statues includes passing their children through the red hot arms or shaken over the idol god Molech, of the Ammonites, the same as the Egyptian sun god Amun-ra, and also called Chemosh by the Moabites. The hollowed statue was placed upon a pedestal of brass, the head was crowned, and resembled a calf. The arms were extended to receive it's victims. The Statue was near hellishly heated before the dedication ceremony of the children began.

Those that died were considered a sacrifice.

God's such as the Canaanite Ashtoreth, were also worshipped. This female deity, supposedly embodied in the moon, symbolized by a crescent moon across her brow, was a god of fertility. All form of sexual immoralities ran rampant in recognition of her. Ancient idolatrous practices were more vile than most people realize.

The life of Solomon is an excellent example of how depraved and perverted one can become through sin. This man was the recipient of more wisdom and knowledge than any other human being, except, of course, Jesus. God came to Solomon in a dream and granted him his hearts greatest desire. Instead of wishing for wealth or longevity, he asked for wisdom to rule the great nation of Israel. This so impressed God that he granted Solomon unexcelled riches. 1 King 3:5-15. The book of Proverbs was written by a young Solomon. The book of Proverbs can turn a beast into a beauty, a pauper into the prosperous, ignorance into prudence, grotesque into normality, and hate into heart-rendering unconditional love. This book can show us the way to loving, lasting marriages and help us raise moral and dedicated children. These precious ancient writings also can help us to live long, flourishing, and enjoyable lives.

The paralleled lives of the two Solomon's, (the young and the old), is astoundingly contrasted. Imagine a man with such impeccable wisdom, degrading himself down to a point of murder and possibly homosexuality. These sins were the end result of his participation with his pagan wives in these disillusioned but vile "religious" practices.

Sin is likened unto leaven, Matt. 16:6-12; Luke 12:1; and 1 Cor. 5:8. The snowball affect of these idolatrous acts swelled and soon overcame the powerful nation to a consummation of civil war. After the death of Solomon, those who wished to remain in idolatry migrated to the north and formed a new nation, commonly referred to in scripture (chronically after 1 King 12), as "Israel" or "Ephraim." Those that wished to remain loyal to Jehovah remained and formed "Judah" also commonly referred to as "Benjamin" in scriptures.

All the kings of the northern tribes were evil. The northern half of this once great and moral nation eventually fell into the hands of the powerful but evil empire of Assyria. the Assyrians dispersed the Israelites into many diverse lands and brought people of other conquered lands into the area in an effort to control rebellion. Thus, they eventually became the hated Samaritans of Jesus' day. They weren't considered pure blooded Jews and were heavily ostracized by the religious Pharisees and Saducees.

Some of the southern kings tried to steer Judah back to morality. Hezekiah and Josiah attempted brave reforms, but the damage had been done, it was too late, sin had its fiendish grip. Some two hundred years after the northern tribes fell to Assyria, the southern tribes succumbed to Nebuchadezzar and the overwhelming dominance of the Babylonians. The Jews remained in captivity for seventy years until Artaxerxes, king of Persia, granted them freedom. Israel, though, was never able to retain their former glory, wealth, or military might that they obtained under King David or Solomon.

Blessings for Obedience

Many are the examples of God blessing brave, obedient, and moral men. Oh, how we need the courage of

Noah, as he consistently stood in the faces of criticism and ridicule while building an ark (rather a barge) to rise above a flood, where in, it had not once rained.

Having the faith of Abraham, when he placed his promised son Isaac upon a sacrificial alter, relying only upon the promise of God, would forever close the gates of hell.

If we would strive to obtain and observe God's wisdom, such as did the young Solomon, and let loose of our obstinacy, then Christianity would shine as a gem in the ruff. The world would soon be taken by the love, joy, and long suffering examples empowered to us by the same power that created it all in the very beginning, the omnipotent Holy Spirit.

> Genesis 1:2
> "AND THE EARTH WAS WITHOUT FORM, AND VOID; AND DARKNESS WAS UPON THE FACE OF THE DEEP. AND THE SPIRIT MOVED UPON THE FACE OF THE WATERS."

We need the dedication of the prophet Daniel, whose prayers, for thirty days, were made illegal under punishment resulting in the lion's den. He boldly left open his window, kneeling three times a day, giving thanks, as he did before. This kind of dedication would so passionately move God to answer salvation prayers, that none would have to be eternally lost. Daniel chapter 6.

David was said to be a man after God's own heart. Acts 13:22. What does it take for a man to receive such a compliment of compliments from God? One must just obey the first and second commandments given by Jesus.

Mark 12:30-31
"AND THOU SHALT LOVE THE LORD THY GOD
WITH ALL THY HEART, AND WITH ALL THY SOUL,
AND WITH ALL THY MIND AND WITH ALL THY
STRENGTH; THIS IS THE FIRST COMMANDMENT.
"AND THE SECOND IS LIKE, NAMELY THIS, THOU
SHALT LOVE THY NEIGHBOR AS THY SELF."

David truly did love God with all his heart, mind, soul,
and strength. David committed adultery and murder.
He was disobedient on numerous occasions, but, he
wasn't just sorry for the results of his sin, but was sincerely sorry for his sins, all because of his great love for
his Holy God.
David's love for God is plenty evident in his writings of
the inspiring book of Psalms.

Psalms 9:1
"I WILL PRAISE THEE, O LORD WITH MY WHOLE
HEART; I WILL SHEW FORTH ALL THY MARVEL-
OUS WORKS."

Psalms 13:5
"BUT I HAVE TRUSTED IN THY MERCY; MY
HEART SHALL REJOICE IN THY SALVATION."

Psalms 40:8
"I DELIGHT TO DO THY WILL, O MY GOD; YEA,
THY LAW IS WITHIN MY HEART."

Psalms 51:10-12
"CREATE IN ME A CLEAN HEART, O GOD, AND
RENEW A RIGHT SPIRIT WITHIN ME."

"CAST ME NOT AWAY FROM THY PRESENCE;
AND TAKE NOT THY HOLY SPIRIT FROM ME."
"RESTORE UNTO ME THE JOY OF THY SALVA-
TION AND UPHOLD ME WITH THY FREE SPIRIT."

Psalms 57:7
"MY HEART IS FIXED, O GOD, MY HEART IS
FIXED; I WILL SING AND GIVE PRAISE."

Psalms 119:11
"THY WORD HAVE I HID IN MINE HEART, THAT I
MIGHT NOT SIN AGAINST THEE."

Psalms 119:161
"PRINCES HAVE PERSECUTED ME WITHOUT A
CAUSE; BUT MY HEART STANDETH IN AWE OF
THY WORD."

Psalms 129:23-24
"SEARCH ME, O GOD, AND KNOW MY HEART;
TRY ME, AND KNOW MY; THOUGHTS."
"AND SEE IF THERE BE ANY WICKED WAY IN
ME, AND LEAD ME IN THE WAY EVERLASTING."

When we are sincerely in love with God as David was,
and love all races, creeds, and colors, as ourselves, then
when we do sin against either, then we will experience
unfeigned and sincere Godly sorrow. The kind of sorrow
that works toward repentance. 2 Corinthians 7:10.

Matthew 7:12
"THEREFORE ALL THINGS WHATSOEVER YE
WOULD THAT MAN SHOULD DO TO YOU, DO YE

EVEN SO TO THEM; FOR THIS IS THE LAW AND
THE PROPHETS.

Matthew 22:40
"ON THESE TWO COMMANDMENTS HANG ALL
THE LAW AND THE PROPHETS."

Loving unconditionally is the golden key to God's heart.
Wholeheartedly dedicating our lives to God and the bet-
terment of all God's people brings everything else into a
joyous and jubilant excellence. When we learn to unconditionally love, then we are yielding to the Holy Spirit,
and then we will experience his undiminished and pure
love.

Reading and understanding the Old Testament is far
as the east from the west from being a waste of our Christian time. It's the desire of God for us to pore over, com-
prehend, believe, and dwell in his unadulterated and
unabated word. All 66 books have accessible treasures
for the soul, mind, and flesh.

-The numeric value of the Hebrew word for Jehovah is 26, equivalent to the number of Bible writers.

-The numeric value of the names of all 26 writers is
7,931 (7x1,333).

-The numeric value of the Old testament writers is
3,808 (7x544). Leaving the New Testament writers with a numeric value of 4,123 (7x589).

In the original Hebrew Canon the books appear in a

different order than those in modern Bible versions. Therefore, because of this re-arrangement several numeric schemes were destroyed.

Original Book Order

The Hebrew Bible fell into seven main divisions.

(1) Law
1. Genesis
2. Exodus
3. Leviticus
4. Numbers
5. Deuteronomy

(2) Prophetic
6. Joshua
7. Judges
8. 1 Samuel
9. 2 Samuel
10. 1 Kings
11. 2 Kings
12. Isaiah
13. Jeremiah
14. Ezekiel
15. Hosea
16. Joel
17. Amos
18. Obadiah
19. Jonah
20. Micah
21. Nahum
22. Habakkuk
23. Zephaniah
24. Haggai
25. Zechariah
26. Malachi

(3) Writings
27. Psalms
28. Proverbs
29. Job
30. Song of Solomon
31. Ruth
32. Lamentations
33. Ecclesiastes
34. Esther
35. Daniel
36. Ezra
37. Nehemiah
38. 1 Chronicles
39. 2 Chronicles

(4) Gospels
40. Matthew
41. Mark
42. Luke
43. John

(5) Acts
44. Acts

(6) Epistles
45. James
46. 1 Peter
47. 2 Peter
48. 1 John
49. 2 John
50. 3 John
51. Jude
52. Romans
53. 1 Corinthians
54. 2 Corinthians
55. Galatians
56. Ephesians
57. Philippians
58. Colossians
59. 1 Thessalonians
60. 2 Thessalonians
61. Hebrews
62. 1 Timothy
63. 2 Timothy
64. Titus
65. Philemon

(7) Revelation
66. Revelation

Writer Numerics

-Moses' and John's names (the first and last writers) have a combined numeric value of 1,414
(7x202).

-The names of the writers between Moses and John
have a numeric value of 6,517 (7x931).

-The names of the writers from Moses to Malachi
(Law and Prophets) have anumeric value of 2,933
(7x419).

-The names of the writers from Psalms to 2
Chronicles (writings) have a combined numeric
value of 875 (7x125).

-David's name occurs 1,134 times throughout the
Old and New Testaments (7x162).

-Moses' name occurs 847 times throughout the
scriptures (7x121).

Enjoy these ingenious validating mathematical
schemes of 11's.

-66 books (11x6).

-44 books have accredited (non-anonymous) writers (11x4); and 22 are non-accredited (11x2).

-Of the 44 accredited books, 22 (11x2), belong to

the writers of more than one book.

-33 books have epistles (contain or are letters) and 33 have none (11x3).

-The Apostle Paul was accredited for writing the most books. His name has a numeric value of 781 (11x71).

Appearance Order Number

The appearance order number will be referred to as (AON) from here-on, is God's assigned order number for each book. (Examples: Genesis is the first book in the order of the 66 books, Exodus the second, Leviticus the third and etc.....)

-The sum of all the AON's of all 66 books is 2,211 (11x201).

-The 22 books of the authors of more than one book have an (AON sum of 946 (11x86) and the other 44 books have an (AON) sum of 1,265 (11x115).

-The (AON) sum of the epistle books is 1,155 (11x105); leaving the non-epistle books with a sum of 1,056 (11x96).

-The first, middle, and last epistle books have an (AON) sum of 165 (11x15).

-The first and last epistle books have an (AON) of 110 (11x10).

-The middle epistle has an (AON) of 55 (11x5).

-The seven great division of Bible books begin with Genesis, Joshua, Psalms, Matthew, Acts, James, and Revelation. They end with Deuteronomy, Malachi, 2 Chronicles, John, Acts, Philemon, and Revelation. Respectively, the (AON's) of these books are 1, 5, 6, 26, 27, 39, 40, 43, 44, 45, 65, 66 for a combined sum of 407 (11x37).

-Moses' name appears 847 times is also a multiple of 11 as well as 7 (11x77) (7x121).

-Moses' name appears less than 10 times in 21 different books. His name occurs a sum of 77 times in these 21 books (11x7).

-In books where is name appears more than 10 times, his name occurs 770 times (11x70) and (11x7x10).

-The non-epistles have Moses' name 825 times (11x75) and 22 times in the epistles (11x2).

Once more be reminded, there are over 31,000 verses of Holy Scripture, and all ordained with these supremely deployed and extraordinary numeric designs. Over 40,000 numeric designs were documented by Dr. Ivan Panin through his tireless labors. In the fifty something years since his death this work has continued with even more astonishing and converting God created numerics uncovered.

Chapter 6
A New Beginning

I am praying as a result of this work, you the reader, if you have not already allowed Jesus to be Savior and Lord of your life, will sincerely soon do so.

I am praying that God will reveal unto you the impossibility of man to articulate all these mathematical wonderments. God prepared all this for your benefit. I have heard it said ever so many times that God moves in mysterious ways, but most of the time if we think in the direction of eternal life, keeping our minds and hearts on the things above, then we'll begin to understand the mind of God a little better, and some of the mystique will start to dissipate.

Humans have a tendency to have only earthly visions and aspirations, but God never, ever takes his eyes of eternity.

Matthew 16:26
"FOR WHAT IS A MAN PROFITED, IF HE SHALL GAIN THE WHOLE WORLD, AND LOST HIS OWN SOUL? OR WHAT SHALL A MAN GIVE IN EXCHANGE FOR HIS SOUL."

By now even the most zealous of skeptics are apprehensively but disquietly curious. Some will theorize methods to dispute and disprove these convincing and converting mathematical phenomena. These skeptics will search negatively, trying to find mathematical schemes that don't exist, where they think they should. Even if some schemes seem less than complete, one you can't ignore the many that are. Say for instance, since the first verse of Genesis contains three nouns, God, heaven, and Earth, with a numeric value of 777, should anyone try to discredit the numeric schemes of Gen. 1:1 because they find another verse with the God in it that concerns creation that doesn't have a numeric value of 777?

Examine the numerics of the Antediluvian Patriarchs, and the seven multiples of seven given in chapter two of this book. If any of their names failed to be a multiple of seven does that annual the previous mathematical concepts?

Suppose another name for Satan was found to have a numeric value that was not a multiple of 13; does that diminish the odds of the six features offered in chapter three of them being just happenstance? 1 in (13x13x13x13x13x13) or 1 in 4,826,822.

The random chances of any numeric feature being a multiple of 13 is 1 in 13. The random chances of any two multiples of 13 would simply and naturally be 13 to the second power, and so on.

The larger the number the less odds are of it appearing as a multiple. The numbers 37 and 73 were used quite extensively by God in Biblical mathematics, each being a non-multiple of no other number.

Far from being wholly intact, I have illustrated how several mathematical concepts are undeniably coherent and correlated through these chapters. If the portrayal of consonants and vowels was just patchwork found only, for instance, in the genealogy of Christ, then it would be easier for one to assume happenstance. Not only are these vowels and consonants found in multiples of seven in Matthew 1:1-11, but God also established relevance in Matthew 1:18-25 (the angel's announcement of Christ), in Mark 1:1-8 (the prophesy of Jesus's ministry from john the Baptist), and in Mark 16:9-20. In all four occurrences both vowels and consonants added up to be multiples of seven. They also added up in the vocabulary words as multiples of seven.

Illustrated in these chapters is how God set forth in detail, words in key areas in multiples of seven. Genesis 1:1 has 7 words, the entire first chapter of Genesis has 434 words, (7x61); Announcement of Christ by the angel has 161 words. Matthew 1;18-25, (7x23). Matthew chapter 2 (childhood of Jesus) also has 161 words. The angel spoke 77 vocabulary words in Jesus's birth announcement. John the Baptist spoke 77 vocabulary words in his prophecy of Jesus' ministry. In the announcement of the church 77 vocabulary words were spoken. In the heavily disputed last twelve verses of Mark, there are 175 words (7x25), and Jesus spoke 42 (7x6) vocabulary words addressing his disciples.

Throughout these chapters I've also recorded how God numbered letters in similar ways as multiples of 7, 11, and 4. Genesis has 28 letters, God, heaven and earth have 14 letters. First three words of Genesis 1:1 have 14 letters, the 4th and 5th words have 7 letters, the 6th and 7th have 7 letters and the last 4 words have 14 letters. The first 4 words have 16 letters and the last 3 words have 12 letters and the first and last two words have 16 letters.

In Matthew 1:1-11 the first three words have 21 letters and the last 4 have 28 letters. In Matthew 1:18-25 (Jesus' angelic birth announcement) there are 396 letters, (11x36); the number of letters beginning with consonants is 253, (11 x23) and beginning with vowels are 143 letters, (11x 13). In Matthew chapter 2, Jesus' childhood, the 77 vocabulary words have 896 letters. (7x128); in Mark 16:9-20, there are 98 vocabulary words with 533 letters, (7x79).

How God ingeniously assigned Bible books certain appearance order numbers coordinating with multiples of 11's is nothing short of absolutely astonishing. Last but certainly not least astonishing to me, is the fact that the man that God anointed to write the most of all the authors, the Apostle Paul, has a 781 numeric value name, which is also a multiple of eleven, (11x71).

God profoundly and incontestably incorporated the numeral seven to single out the congruence and oneness of all Bible writers. The numeric value of all 26 writers' names is 7,931, (7x1,333). The writers of the law and prophetic books have a numeric value of 2,993, (7x419). The writers of the writings have a numeric value of 875, (7x125); and all the Old Testament writers have 3,808, (7x544) for their value. The New Testament writers' names have a combined numeric value of 4,123, (7x587).

Embarking seemingly on impossibility, all seven forms of the Hebrew name Jeremiah have a combined numeric value of 1,953, (7x279). All seven forms occur 147 times in scriptures, (7x21); and adding all occurrences you have a numeric value sum of 39,865, (7x5,695).

Convincing enough in itself, the entire Hebrew alphabet sums up to 1,495, the same number of years Israel struggled under law. The entire Greek alphabet has a sum of 3,999, from the birth of Adam to the birth of Christ.

The awe-inspiring coherence of these well organized mathematical factors are undeniable and uncompromising. Even if the most radical and relentless extremists try to find quote, "any areas of inconsistencies," they will most likely outline even further mathematical blueprints.

Bible Points To

The Bible points to and centers around Jesus. The Old Testament not only contains hundreds of prophecies of Him, but flourishes with thousand of symbolic types.

If Jesus was removed from the scriptures, as the Son of God, then the Bible would be just another historical writing. The things that God asked of Moses, Abraham, and other anointed servants would seem as foolishness if some future atonement was not eminent. The temple furnishings and the ark of the covenant both contain crystal clear implications to the futuristic savior and blood atonement. The procedures required for the sacrifice of the animals are more than pertinent in relevancy to Jesus' sacrificial death. The asking of Abraham to lay his own son on the altar as a burnt offering would deem God cruel and paganish were not as a type of the coming Messiah.

Furthermore, if Jesus didn't come in the time period He did, most of the prophecies pertaining to him could never have been fulfilled. If he isn't the Son of God, then the whole Bible is full of mistakes.

The pinnacle of perfection; hundreds of prophecies, thousands of symbolic types, embellished with innumerable mathematics, and millions that can testify to metamorphic conversions. The evidence is overwhelming! The path to eternal life is perpetually prepared. We can now choose life through Him, Christ our Lord.

Not once, has it been exhibited, throughout the entirety of this script, is the degree of numeric saturation that God actually embedded in any area of His Holy Word.

Prayerfully feeling constrained by God's most Holy Spirit to present enough numeric evidence to convince, the Spirit now predispositions me to conclude this chapter with an in-depth illustration of just how the Bible truly is exceedingly saturated with numerics. This illustration, though, by no means is 100% complete, just in-depth.

Jesus stated in John 6:48 that He was the bread of life. The bible states in 1 John 5:12 that he who has the Son has life. Jesus is connected with life in scores of places throughout the scriptures.

> John 14:6
> "JESUS SAITH UNTO HIM, I AM THE WAY, THE TRUTH, AND THE LIFE; NO MAN COMETH UNTO THE FATHER, BUT BY ME."

Bold statement made by only one Holy man, but God the Son has all the backing he could ever need from God the Father. Just as Noah, his wife, his sons, and their wives were eight people that were chosen to re-establish life on earth, Christ was chosen to re-establish eternal life, for Gentile and Jew alike, in heaven. God symbolically chose eight people, just like he chose the Greek alphabet and the number eight, seven times, to prove, yet another way, to the world that Jesus was God incarnated.

Jesus, the Christ, Savior, Lord, Messiah, the Son of man, and the Truth are all divisible by the number eight.

Eight is a number used of God to represent a new beginning. Through the blood that was shed and spilled at Calvary, if we so chose, can all begin new. Even though our sins are as red as scarlet and are as filthy as menstruous rags, we can be made whole, clean and white in the eyes of God as new pure fallen snow.

Eternal Life

John 14:26
"BUT THE COMFORTER, WHICH IS THE HOLY GHOST, WHOM THE FATHER WILL SEND IN MY NAME, HE SHALL TEACH YOU ALL THINGS, AND BRING ALL THINGS TO YOUR REMEMBRANCE, WHATSOEVER I HAVE SAID UNTO YOU."

God the Holy Spirit is who regenerates us, quickens our spirits, and circumcises the hearts unto the born again experience.

-The Greek word "pneuma" is used for life and also translates spirit (used with Holy Spirit), the word has a numeric value of 576, (8x72).

-The phrase "breath of Jehovah" in Judges 3:10, has a numeric value of 240, (8x30).

Genesis 3:22
"AND THE LORD SAID THE MAN HAS BECOME ONE OF US, TO KNOW GOOD AND EVIL; AND NOW, LEST HE PUT FORTH HIS HAND, AND TAKE ALSO THE TREE OF LIFE, AND EAT AND LIVE FOREVER"

-The phrase, "the tree of life and live forever," has a numeric value of 480, (8x60).

-The words "and live" have a numeric value of **24, (8x3).**

Genesis 3:24
"SO HE DROVE OUT THE MAN: AND PLACED AT THE EAST OF THE GARDEN OF EDEN CHERUBIMS, AND A FLAMING SWORD WHICH TURNED EVERY WAY, TO KEEP THE WAY TO THE TREE OF LIFE."

-"and a flaming sword which turned every way" has a numeric value of 1,200 (8x150).

-"and a flaming sword which turned every way, to keep the way of the tree of "life" has a numeric value of 2,400, (8x300).

Exceptional and incredible as these six features of multiples of eight are correlated and synchronized with Hebrew phrases and the Greek word "pneuma" concerning life, but outright unforgettable is the fact that this synchronization and correlation befalls upon the Greek as well as the Hebrew writings.

Revelation 2:7
"HE THAT HATH AN EAR, LET HIM EAR WHAT THE SPIRIT SAITH UNTO THE CHURCHES; TO HIM THAT OVERCOMETH WILL I GIVE TO EAT OF THE TREE OF LIFE, WHICH IS IN THE MIDST OF THE PARADISE OF GOD."

-The phrase "to him that overcometh will I give to eat of the tree of life," has a numeric value of 6,240, (8x780).

-"to eat of the tree of life which is in the midst of the paradise of God" has a numeric value of 7,200, (8x900).

-"the tree of life which is" has a numeric value of 3,120, (8x390).

-"him that overcometh" has a numeric value of 2,400, (8x300).

-The word tree has a numeric value of 960, (8x120).

Revelation 22:2
'IN THE MIDST OF THE STREET OF IT, AND ON EITHER SIDE OF THE RIVER, WAS THERE THE TREE OF LIFE, WHICH BARE TWELVE MANNER OF FRUITS, AND YIELDED HER FRUIT EVERY MONTH: AND THE LEAVES OF THE TREES WERE FOR THE HEALING OF THE NATIONS."

-"the leaves of the trees" has a numeric value of 1,920, (8x240).

-"of the tree" has a numeric value of 960, (8x120).

-"the leaves" has a numeric value of 960, (8x120).

-"on either side of the river" has a numeric value of

960, (8x120).

Revelation 22:14
"BLESSED ARE THEY THAT DO HIS COMMAND-
MENTS, THAT THEY MAY HAVE RIGHT TO THE
TREE OF LIFE, AND MAY ENTER IN THROUGH
THE GATES INTO THE CITY."

-"that they may have right to the tree of life" has a
numeric value of 5,040, (8x630).

-"that they might have the right" has a numeric
value of 2,400, (8x300).

-"the city" has a numeric value of 240 (8x30).

Matthew 12:33
"EITHER MAKE THE TREE GOOD, AND HIS FRUIT
GOOD, OR ELSE MAKE THE TREE CORRUPT:
FOR THE TREE IS KNOWN BY HIS FRUIT."

-"a tree is known" has a numeric value of 1,680,
(8x210).

-"his fruit" has a numeric value of 1,440, (8x180).

John 3:3
"JESUS ANSWERED AND SAID UNTO HIM, VER-
ILY, VERILY, I SAY UNTO THEE, EXCEPT A MAN
BE BORN AGAIN, HE CANNOT SEE THE KING-
DOM OF GOD."

2 Corinthians 5:17
"THEREFORE IF ANY MAN BE IN CHRIST, HE IS A NEW CREATURE' OLD THINGS ARE PASSED AWAY; BEHOLD, ALL THINGS ARE BECOME NEW."

Romans 10:9-10
"THAT IF THOU SHALL CONFESS WITH THY MOUTH THE LORD JESUS, AND SHALT BELIEVE IN THINE HEART THAT GOD HAS RAISED HIM FROM THE DEAD, THOU SHALT BE SAVED." "FOR WITH THE HEART MAN BELIEVETH UNTO RIGHTEOUSNESS; AND WITH THE MOUTH CON-FESSION IS MADE UNTO SALVATION."

St. John 3:8
"THE WIND BLOWETH WHERE IT LISTETH AND THOU HEAREST THE SOUND THEREOF BUT CANST NOT TELL WHENCE IT COMETH, AND WITHER IT GOETH: SO IS EVERY ONE THAT IS BORN OF THE SPIRIT."

-The phrase "born of the Spirit" has a numeric value of 2,304, (8x288).

I've countless times heard the words of Jesus "born again" mocked and ridiculed, but just in case you're wondering;

-"born again" has a numeric value of 176, (8x22).

Chapter 7
Numerics Plus

Numerics are not the only evidence offered of God that substantiates that the Bible is Godly inspired. In my opinion though, I think numerics are a very enticing and decisive tool. Numerics don't favor any particular doctrines, theories, or beliefs. Numerics cross language barriers, and if we were to ever communicate with "life" beyond this planet it would probably have to be through the universal language of mathematics.

The fact that God laced every verse, (over 31,100), goes beyond any chance of intelligent denial. I imagine though, there will be "intelligent" people that still will turn their backs to a loving Savior amid all of this immeasurable and stunning evidence.

God also elected proof of the scientific, prophetic, and the ELC (equi-distant letter sequences) nature. Today's archaeological findings have proven, in the eyes of most, such things as the existence of King David, the disputed existence of Biblical cities, and found evidences of supposedly never existing Biblical nations.

The title of this book though, is *Undeniable Proofs*. The evidences that have been presented, maybe at the risk of sounding a little arrogant, but welcoming all challenges, I think are truly undeniable. It is for that reason, undeniable proofs, that this chapter will not contain validations from the field of Archaeology. Note I used the word "validations," because I love archaeology and strongly believe in the proof it offers. I think most if not all scientific minded people would agree. Although, it may at times seem so, this book was not written just for scientific minded folk. There are some who dismiss archaeological evidences as "educated guess work."

This guideline will not only apply to the field of archaeology, but to certain prophecies and scientific proofs as well.

Scientific Proof

Isaiah 40:22
"IT IS HE THAT SITTETH UPON THE CIRCLE OF THE EARTH, AND THE INHABITANTS THEREOF ARE AS GRASSHOPPERS; THAT STRETCHETH OUT THE HEAVENS AS A CURTAIN, AND SPEADETH THEM OUT AS A TENT TO DWELL IN.,"

Proverbs 8:27
"WHEN HE PREPARED THE HEAVENS I WAS THERE: WHEN HE SET A COMPASS UPON THE FACE OF THE DEPTH:"

Twice the Bible recorded the fact the Earth was spherical. The first time man had any inclination the world was not flat, and the sun and stars didn't rotate around Earth was in the seventh century B.C. The Greek astronomer Thales noticed that the Big Dipper constellation, in Greece, never fell below the horizon as it did in Egypt. Anaximander, a student of Thales, legend has it, realized the earth must be spherical. Although, others through different means, throughout the centuries came to the same conclusions. Not until 1492 was the fact settled once and for all.

The book of Isaiah was originally recorded around 800

B.C. and Proverbs around 1000 B.C., the latter was nearly three hundred years before science even began to catch up with ancient God inspired Biblical wisdom.

Jeremiah 33.26
"AS THE HOST OF HEAVEN CANNOT BE NUM-BERED, NEITHER THE SANDS OF THE SEAS MEASURED:"

Not only here, but in other scriptures, the Bible compares the stars with the sands of the seas centuries before any telescope was invented. Approximately three thousand stars can be counted with the naked eye.

Only recently has science classified the universe as infinite over 2500 years after this Bible passage.

Job 38:16
"HAS THOU ENTERED INTO THE SPRINGS OF THE SEA? OR HAST THOU WALKED IN THE SEARCH OF THE DEPTH."

Our modern sonar equipment has allowed us to "walk" the depths of the seas and we have discovered there truly are springs and water channels in the deep. Until just very recently man considered the ocean floor deep, sandy, and unrugged. The seas contain mountains, valleys, and a terrain much like dry land.

Job 38: 29-30
"OUT OF WHOSE WOMB CAME THE ICE? AND THE HOARY FROST OF HEAVEN, WHO HATH GENDERED IT?"
"THE WATERS ARE HID AS WITH A STONE, AND

THE FACE OF THE DEEP IS FROZEN."

Just in the last couple of years have we learned that water actually exists in outer-space. comets, meteors, and Mars contain water. Amazingly, we've recently discovered the moon even has a polar cap.

Hebrews 11:3
"THROUGH FAITH WE UNDERSTAND THAT THE WORLDS WERE FRAMED BY THE WORD OF GOD, SO THAT THINGS WHICH ARE SEEN WERE NOT MADE OF THINGS WHICH DO APPEAR."

Incredible as it is, the Bible actually refers to molecules and atoms. In this verse of Hebrews, we're told the worlds are made of things that do not appear or rather cannot be seen.

Hygienic, sanitary, and dietary laws of the Bible were nearly 3,000 years ahead of their time. The ancient Israelites were given commandments for reasons that only modern science could understand. Although, I'm not going to detail about them, critics will argue that this wisdom was the result of trial and error. If that is the case, then will someone please tell me why no other nation learned in this manner. Even in modern times some nations are still ignorant of these health and life saving commandments.

Prophetic Proof

Revelation 13:16-17
"AND HE CAUSETH ALL BOTH SMALL AND GREAT, RICH AND POOR, FREE AND BOND, TO

RECEIVE A MARK IN THEIR RIGHT HAND, OR IN
THIER FOREHEADS."
"AND THAT NO MAN MIGHT BUY OR SELL, SAVE
HE THAT HAD THE MARK, OR THE NAME OF
THE BEAST, OR THE NUMBER OF HIS NAME."

These scriptures were written in 90 A.D., nearly 2,000
years before anyone could ever dream that such power
could be levied and enforced. Never in the history of
man could anyone exert such authority.

As we are rapidly emerging into the twenty-first century, we now can see this is a real distinct possibility.

A cashless society would not be hard to sell. The ben-
efits would be no bad checks, fewer robberies, almost
kill the drug cartel, and with a personal identification
system fraud would almost be nonexistent.

With computers being obsolete almost on a yearly ba-
sis, we can clearly and easily see the technology needed
to control all monetary transactions is not just some futuristic fantasy.

Ezekiel 26:14
"AND I WILL MAKE THEE LIKE THE TOP OF A
ROCK: THOU SHALT BE A PLACE TO SPREAD
NETS UPON; THOU SHALT BE BUILT NO MORE:
FOR I THE LORD HAVE SPOKEN IT, SAITH THE
LORD GOD."

The ancient city of Tyre was a major port city of biblical
times. As in any ancient sea port, wealth and idolatry
flourished and was unrestrained. The old Testament
prophet Ezekiel prophesied in vivid detail an up-coming
complete destruction of this ancient city if there was not

repentance.

Ezekiel warned them their city would be made flat as a rock and the stones and timbers would be thrown into the sea.

When the citizens of Tyre knew they were soon to be under the siege of Nebuchadnezzar and his mighty Babylonian empire, they moved by ship, to a neighboring island about a half-mile off their coast. When Nebuchadnezzar found the city moved and empty he completely destroyed it, but the people survived out of his reach since he had no naval forces.

Some 250 years later the city of Tyre had a rift with Alexander the Great, who took the ruins of the old mainland city and constructed a causeway out to the island. Attacking from the sea side with his newly developed naval power and causeway, Alexander was able to subdue the fortified island city.

Ezekiel's prophetical words have far more range than just the sieges of Nebuchadnezzar and Alexander the Great. He also proclaimed the city never again would exalt to it's former reputation and renown. He accurately fore-told of the island's modern day modest fishing village.

Amos 1:8
"AND I WILL CUT OFF THE INHABITANT FROM ASHDOD, AND HIM THAT HIDETH THE SCEPTRE FROM ASHEKON, AND I WILL TURN MINE HAND AGAINST EKRON; AND THE REMNANT OF THE PHILISTINES WILL PERISH, SAITH THE LORD GOD."

The Philistine people were avaricious enemies of the Israelites as they first attempted entry into the promise land. Numerous times, as a resulting judgement for sin, the Israelites were enslaved by the Philistines. The Philistines, excessively cruel, and with unwarranted ruthlessness persecuted God's people despite and in the midst of phrophetical warnings.

Today, though, the Philistine people have no descendants. Their nationality as well as their race is now prophetically extinct.

The Amaleks were another nation and race that were issued the prophetic ax. They cowardly attacked the Israelites from the rear when they were weary and weak from their strenuous wilderness travels (Ex. 17:8-13; Duet. 25:17-19; and 1 Cor. 4:39-43).

In Matthew chapter 24 Jesus was asked by his disciples for signs of the end times. He told them of false messiahs, rumors of wars, kingdoms against kingdoms, famines, pestilences, earthquakes, persecuted Christians and love waxing cold because of lawlessness.

I've personally heard hard-core skeptics attack this prophetic passage of our Lord and Savior by saying these conditions are as old as the world itself. They are right, to some degree, we have seen false messiahs, had our "police actions" and fought major wars, experienced famines, pestilence's, and earthquakes. I doubt that there has been a Christian generation pass since the crucifixion of Christ that has not endured persecution. Fear has been striking men's hearts from the beginning. Until this generation we've seen these things happen sporadically. Since the fifties, however, there has been a dramatic increase in all areas of these prophecies. Jesus also talked of one generation seeing all these increased events.

I'm not 100% advocating this as the last generation,

simply because we've been warned against such teachings, but on the other hand I would not be taken by surprise whatsoever at all. I'll say this without reservations, if this isn't the generation that will experience our Lord's return, I'm surely blessed to live at this time, because if it is to be worse that what were presently experiencing, then it would have to be as we've seen in moves such as *The Terminator* and other pay television productions that portray a deplorable and wretched society.

2 Timothy 3: 1-5
"THIS KNOW ALSO THAT IN THE LAST DAYS PERILOUS TIMES SHALL COME."
"FOR MEN SHALL BE LOVERS OF THEIR OWN SELVES, COVETOUS, BOASTERS, PROUD, BLASPHEMERS, DISOBEDIENT TO PARENTS, UNTHANKFUL, UNHOLY,"
"WITHOUT NATURAL AFFECTION, TRUCE BREAKERS, FALSE ACCUSERS, INCONTINENT, FIERCE, DESPISERS OF THOSE THAT ARE GOOD."
"TRAITORS, HEADY, HIGHMINDED, LOVERS OF PLEASURES, MORE THAN LOVERS OF GOD;"
"HAVING A FORM OF GODLINESS, BUT DENYING THE POWER THEREOF; FROM SUCHTURN AWAY."

To my knowledge, there's never been a time in recorded history, other than the twentieth century, that satanic worship and witchcraft were tolerated.

Satanist have built "churches," manipulated their way into prisons, and have demanded their rights under the guise of religion. As long as they quote "break no laws," they have the blessings of our federal government.

The worship of ancient idols parallels modern Satan worship to an astounding degree, both practice animal and human sacrifices and sexual contact with each other and demonic spirits. The more established groups have "specified breeders," women that bear children solely for sacrificial purposes. These infants and young children are lain upon the altar and serve as a burnt offering. The residue of body fat is then used to make their candles.

Ancient man had no inclination that he was in fact practicing satanic worship, but modern man knows that idol gods were nothing more than myth and satanic lies.

Equi-distant Letter Sequences

Equi-distance letter sequences (ELS) is a method used to find hidden codes or messages in the ancient manuscripts. The way it works is that a person will start with a particular Hebrew alphabetical letter, then he/she may go to, for instance, every seventh letter, recording each one until a Hebrew word is discovered. The procedure works either left to right or right to left. Jewish Rabbis have entered copies of the ancient Hebrew text through series of computer searches to uncover these hidden words and messages of God.

In the very first verse of the Bible (Hebrew texts) starting with the Hebrew alphabetical letter "yod" in the Hebrew word "b raisheet" counting every 521st letter eight times left to right, we'll find the Hebrew words, "Yeshua yahkol," which translates into English as "Yeshua" "Jesus "yahkol" is able. By the way, 521 is the numeric value for the Hebrew word for gift.

Isaiah 53:10
"YET IT PLEASED THE LORD TO BRUISE HIM;

HE HATH PUT HIM TO GRIEF: WHEN THOU
SHALT MAKE HIS SOUL AN OFFERING FOR SIN,
HE SHALL SEE HIS SEED, HE SHALL PROLONG
HIS DAYS, AND THE PLEASURE OF THE LORD
SHALL PROSPER IN HIS HANDS."

Starting with the sixth to the last Hebrew "yod" of this
verse, counting every 20th letter seven time from left to
right, we find the phrase "Yeshua (Jesus) is my name."
   In almost every exemplar Old Testament prophecy of
Jesus, Yeshua or other relating words or phrases can be
found.

Isaiah 61:1-2
"THE SPIRIT OF THE LORD GOD IS UPON ME;
BECAUSE THE LORD HATH ANOINTED ME TO
PREACH GOOD TIDINGS UNTO THE MEEK; HE
HATH SENT ME TO BIND UP THE BROKEN-
HEARTED, TO PROCLAIM LIBERTY TO THE CAP-
TIVES, AND THE OPENING OF THE PRISON TO
THEM THAT ARE BOUND."
"TO PROCLAIM THE ACCEPTABLE YEAR OF THE
LORD."

This prophecy fore-tells of the Holy Spirit anointing
Jesus received and his ministerial work here on earth.
It also fore-tells of his descension into hell to set free Old
Testament saints imprisoned by Satan.
   Starting with the "yod" in the phrase "Spirit of the Lord,"
and every 9th letter left to right seven times, Yeshua
(Jesus) is uncovered again.

Micah 5:2
"BUT THOU, BETHLEHEM EPHRATAH, THOUGH

THOU BE LITTLE AMONG THE THOUSANDS OF
JUDAH, YET OUT OF THEE SHALL HE COME
FORTH UNTO ME THAT IS TO BE RULER IN IS-
RAEL; WHOSE GOINGS FORTH HAVE BEEN
FROM OLD, FROM EVERLASTING."

The Hebrew word Yeshua also is implanted into this
prophecy of Jesus' birthplace. Starting from the fourth
"yod" in this verse, counting every 49th letter four times
left to right.

Zechariah 11:12
"AND I SAID UNTO THEM, IF YE THINK GOOD,
GIVE ME MY PRICE; AND IF NOT, FORBEAR. SO
THEY WEIGHED FOR MY PRICE THIRTY PIECES
OF SILVER."

God implanted Yeshua (Hebrew for Jesus) in this amazing prophecy of Judas Iscariot's betrayal of Jesus for a
mere thirty pieces of silver, starting with the "yod" in
"my price" counting every 24th letter right to left seven
times.

Daniel 9:26
AND AFTER THREESCORE AND TWO WEEKS
SHALL MESSIAH BE CUT OFF, BUT NOT FOR
HIMSELF: AND THE PEOPLE OF THE PRINCE
THAT SHALL COME SHALL DESTROY THE CITY
AND THE SANCTUARY; AND THE END THEREOF
SHALL BE WITH A FLOOD, AND UNTO THE END
OF THE WAR DESOLATIONS ARE DETERMINED."

This verse combined with verse 25, for those who wish
to understand, not only give us prophecy of the messiah's

death (cut-off), but the year it happened 500 years before hand.

Yeshua (Jesus), again, is implanted into this prophetical passage, starting with the "Yod" in "and the city" and
counting every 26th letter left to right three times.

By the way, 26 is the numeric value for the Hebrew
word "Yehovah" or Lord.

> Isaiah 7:14
> "THEREFORE THE LORD HIMSELF SHALL GIVE
> YOU A SIGN; BEHOLD A VIRGIN SHALL CON-
> CEIVE, AND BEAR A SON, AND SHALL CALL HIS
> NAME IMMANUEL."

This hotly contested but center core of Christianity,
the virgin birth prophecy, is heir to the encrypted Hebrew word "Mishiach" (Messiah). From the Hebrew letter "mem" in "virgin" count every 17th letter right to left
three times.

> Psalm 22;16
> "FOR DOGS HAVE COMPASSED: THE ASSEMBLY
> OF THE WICKED HAVE INCLOSED ME: THEY
> PIERCED MY HANDS AND MY FEET."

The punishment of crucifixion was invented by the
Romans some 700 years after these prophecies of Psalms
22. These prophecies go into extensive medical detail
suffered by those who died due to crucifixion. Gradual
fluid build up in the lungs eventually would cause the
crucified's heart to explode. starting from the Hebrew
letter "ayin" counting every 26th letter left to right seven
times uncovers "a sign of Yeshua."

Psalms 22.13
"THEY GAPED UPON ME WITH THEIR MOUTHS,
AS A RAVENING AND A ROARING LION."

"Yeshua cut in pieces," is found encrypted in this verse
by starting with the 2nd letter of the sixth word counting every 26th letter right to left six times. This verse,
like verse 16 of Psalms 22, has 26 intervals, remember
the Hebrew word for Lord "Yehovah" has a numeric value
of 26.

Psalms 22:12
"MANY BULLS HAVE COMPASSED ME: STRONG
BULLS OF BASHAM HAVE BESET ME ROUND."

The Hebrew word for thorns is found encoded into this
scripture, starting with the 1st letter of the 6th word
counting every 3rd letter left to right five times.

Leviticus 21:10
"AND HE THAT IS THE HIGH PRIEST AMONG HIS
BRETHREN, UPON WHOSE HEAD THE ANOINT-
ING OIL WAS POURED, AND THAT IS CONSE-
CRATED TO PUT ON THE GARMENTS, SHALL
NOT UNCOVER HIS HEAD, NOR REND HIS
CLOTHES;"

Chapter 21 of Leviticus lays out the commandments
and statues for the Israeli high priests of Aaron's line.
These men were to live Holy lives, not to defile themselves in paganish practices, marry virgins not whorish
or divorced women, not touch the dead unless they were

close relatives, sin was not to be allowed even from their own children, they were not to mourn, and during any part of the ministering to God in the tabernacle they were allowed no worldly interactions.

The high priest, once a year, would enter into the Most Holy of Holy area of the tabernacle. First he would sprinkle the blood of a bullock, for his own purification, seven times upon the mercy seat eastward. Then he was to kill the goat of the sin offering of the people, carry the blood into the Most Holy of Holy area, and sprinkle it upon the mercy seat eastward seven time. Lev. chapter 16.

Symbolism of Jesus Christ his ministry, and the church is distinct and obvious. The command of God to the priests to live Holy lives is of course, symbolic to the Holy life lived by Jesus. Allowing only the touch of the dead to close relatives is symbolic of believers being part of the family of God, those that chose to remain "spiritually dead" will never touch him. The command not to mourn symbolizes that Christ never saw corruption (bodily decay), and his resurrection. To remain isolated from the secular world during this Holy ritual is to symbolize the blood of Jesus not becoming contaminated, remaining pure for all eternity.

The bullock was an animal the ancients chose when the workload was the most rigorous. The work Christ did, no other man could have fulfilled. Jesus truly carried the weight of the world upon his shoulder, then spilling his blood so the church can follow in his footsteps. The mercy seat is symbolic of the grace or favor we have from the Father through the Son. Sprinkling the blood eastward symbolizes his future appearing in the eastern sky. The high priest only was to kill the goat. The goat is symbolic of Satan, evil, and sin, but the eternal High Priest has overcome Satan, evil, and sin.

The commandment to marry virgins is symbolic of the born again church. The priests not allowing sin even from their own children, symbolizes repentance is an absolute necessity to escape the wages of sin, which is spiritual death and the seperation from God in eternal hell.

In Leviticus chapter 21 verse 10, starting with the first Hebrew "heh" counting every third letter right to left, we can see God implanted, "Behold the blood of Yeshua." The Bible states without the shedding of blood there is not remission of sin. Hebrews 9:22.

Appendix

Bibliography

The Fourth Beast
Howard O. Pittman

The Signature of God
Grant R. Jeffrey

301 Startling Proofs and Prophecies
Peter Lalonde   Paul Lalonde

Verbal Inspiration of the Bible Scientifically Demonstrated
Ivan Panin

The Shorter Works of Ivan Panin
Ivan Panin

Last Twelve Verses of mark
Ivan Panin

Inspiration of the Hebrew Scriptures Scientifically Demonstrated
Ivan Panin

Holy Challenge for Today
Ivan Panin

Dake's Annotated Reference bible
Finis Jennings Dake

Appendix

Theomatics II
Del Washburn

His Name is Jesus
Yacov Rambsel

Yeshua
Yacov Rambsel

Dakes Reference Bible
Finnis Dake